Cambridge Elements ≡

Elements in Politics and Society in East Asia
edited by
Erin Aeran Chung
Johns Hopkins University
Mary Alice Haddad
Wesleyan University
Benjamin L. Read
University of California, Santa Cruz

STATE AND SOCIAL PROTESTS IN CHINA

Yongshun Cai
Hong Kong University of Science and Technology
Chih-Jou Jay Chen
Academia Sinica

CAMBRIDGE
UNIVERSITY PRESS

Shaftesbury Road, Cambridge CB2 8EA, United Kingdom

One Liberty Plaza, 20th Floor, New York, NY 10006, USA

477 Williamstown Road, Port Melbourne, VIC 3207, Australia

314–321, 3rd Floor, Plot 3, Splendor Forum, Jasola District Centre,
New Delhi – 110025, India

103 Penang Road, #05–06/07, Visioncrest Commercial, Singapore 238467

Cambridge University Press is part of Cambridge University Press & Assessment,
a department of the University of Cambridge.

We share the University's mission to contribute to society through the pursuit of
education, learning and research at the highest international levels of excellence.

www.cambridge.org
Information on this title: www.cambridge.org/9781108987301

DOI: 10.1017/9781108982924

© Yongshun Cai and Chih-Jou Jay Chen 2022

This publication is in copyright. Subject to statutory exception and to the provisions of
relevant collective licensing agreements, no reproduction of any part may take place
without the written permission of Cambridge University Press & Assessment.

First published 2022

A catalogue record for this publication is available from the British Library.

ISBN 978-1-108-98730-1 Paperback
ISSN 2632-7368 (online)
ISSN 2632-735X (print)

Cambridge University Press & Assessment has no responsibility for the persistence or
accuracy of URLs for external or third-party internet websites referred to in this
publication and does not guarantee that any content on such websites is, or will
remain, accurate or appropriate.

State and Social Protests in China

Elements in Politics and Society in East Asia

DOI: 10.1017/9781108982924
First published online: October 2022

Yongshun Cai
Hong Kong University of Science and Technology

Chih-Jou Jay Chen
Academia Sinica

Author for correspondence: Yongshun Cai, socai@ust.hk

Abstract: China has witnessed numerous incidents of social protests over the past three decades. Protests create uncertainty for authoritarian governments, and the Chinese government has created, strengthened, and coordinated multiple dispute-resolution institutions to manage social conflicts and protests. Accommodating the aggrieved prevents the accumulation of grievances in society, but concessions require resources. As the frequency and scale of collective action are closely tied to the political opportunity for action, the Chinese government has also contained collective action by shaping the political opportunity available to the aggrieved. This Element shows that when the Chinese central government prioritizes social control, as it has under Xi Jinping's leadership, it signals its preference for stricter social control, and that it will tolerate local governments' use of coercion. As a result, the central and local governments create an environment that is not conducive to the mobilization of collective action. Although reactive collective actions have still occurred in China, large-scale occurrences have been uncommon in recent years.

Keywords: China, conflict, political opportunity, protests, stability

ISBNs: 9781108987301 (PB), 9781108982924 (OC)
ISSNs: 2632-7368 (online), 2632-735X (print)

Contents

1 Introduction

Authoritarian governments exist under the constant threat of mass political unrest. "At any given moment, the public may reject the existing political order and – through action (strikes/protests) in the streets – impose substantial costs upon their leaders, sometimes even ousting the leadership or upending the regime" (Hollyer et al. 2015, 764). In contemporary China, maintaining regime stability has remained the top priority of the party-state. Political challenges, whether originating from political or nonpolitical issues, are not tolerated by the regime. In January 2019, the Chinese Minister of Public Security demanded that the prevention of a "color revolution" become the top priority of the country's police; the infiltration and subversion activities of enemies inside and outside China would need to be curbed, and the leadership of the Party and the socialist system would need to be resolutely defended (Li 2019). Social stability is also seen as crucial to economic development. In 1989 before the Tiananmen movement, Deng Xiaoping (1993) pointed out that if Chinese people protested 365 days a year, it would be impossible to develop the country's economy.

Over the past few decades, the Chinese party-state has allocated a huge amount of resources and manpower to ensure social stability (Chen, Xi 2013). Expenditures on internal security totaled 514 billion yuan in 2009, which is close to the expenditure on national defense, at 480.7 billion yuan;[1] the following year, the former again exceeded the latter (Feng 2018). Maintaining social stability has remained the top priority set for local authorities in China (Edin 2003; Wang 2015). Despite these efforts, incidents of collective action have recurred, though the number of such incidents has varied across time.[2]

The Chinese government's primary approach to ensuring social and political stability is to create what we might call an unorganized society monitored by the party-state. Communist states commonly "organize society in an atomized manner to facilitate control" (Dziak 1988, 168). In an unorganized society, intermediary and independent organizations, such as trade unions or religious organizations, are not allowed to exist. Organizations are often seen as crucial to social movements and collective action. McAdam and Scott (2005, 8) contend that if social movements are to be sustained for any length of time, they "require some form of organization: leadership, administrative structure, incentives for participation, and means for acquiring resources and support." By prohibiting

---

[1] This is reported on a Chinese website. "How Deep Is the Bottomless Hole of the 'Costly Stability Maintenance'" ("天价维稳"的无底洞有多深?), http://opinion.huanqiu.com/1152/2010-06/848498.html.

[2] As discussed later, our data show that incidents of collective action in China reached a peak in 2014 and then began to decline.

such organizations, the authoritarian government deters protest leaders and eradicates mobilization networks, thereby undermining political dissent.

However, social protests in an unorganized society still pose serious challenges to authoritarian rulers. Despite the lack of formal organizations for collective action, mobilization networks are not absent in these regimes. Collective actions in an unorganized society are hard to predict precisely because they are leaderless and spontaneous. Organizations may also emerge during the process of collective action. In addition, new information and communication technologies (ICTs) can help mobilize previously unconnected and unorganized people for collective action (Castells 2015). Moreover, the government's ineffective management of social protests may trigger the escalation or diffusion of collective action, constituting a threat to the regime. Thus, collective action remains a concern for authoritarian governments as long as they are unable to prevent it.

China has witnessed a large number of social conflicts in recent decades due to unprecedented socioeconomic changes that caused grievances among social groups, including employees in the public and private sectors, peasants, home-owners, taxi drivers, veterans, the self-employed, and other urban residents. Although these protests generally focus on issues concerning people's daily lives, they remain a threatening source of social instability due to their possible escalation. Having been assigned the responsibility of maintaining social stability, Chinese local governments have created, strengthened, and coordinated various types of dispute-resolution institutions to ensure local stability. Accommodating certain demands is an important way of appeasing the aggrieved, and this approach prevents the accumulation of grievances in society. But concessions can become too costly for the government. Thus, local responses to social protests vary, ranging from concessions, turning a blind eye, and temporizing, to coercion (Cai 2010; Chen 2012, 2020a; Lee and Zhang 2013; Chen and Chen 2021).

To a large extent, the occurrence and the number of social protests are influenced by the political opportunity available to the aggrieved. This Element examines how the Chinese government has reduced collective action by shaping the political opportunity for collective action. Political opportunity refers to "consistent – but not necessarily formal or permanent – dimensions of the political environment that provide incentives for people to undertake collective action by affecting their expectations for success or failure" (Tarrow 1998, 5). In other words, political opportunity affects the likelihood of collective action by shaping prospective participants' perception about the risk of action and its chance of success.

In China, the political opportunity is shaped by the interaction between the central and local governments. Most Chinese people stage collective action not to challenge the communist regime but to seek redress for specific problems related to their daily lives. Their action is explicitly or implicitly directed at the local government, which is answerable to higher-level authorities, including the central government. Political opportunity for action arises when there are disparities between the central and local authorities. The disparities make people believe that local governments are not allowed to use repression at will or to ignore people's grievances.

By the same token, political opportunities are narrowed or disappear if the central government tolerates the local government's use of repression or when the central government signals its intolerance of social protests. In these circumstances, the disparities between the central and local governments diminish, and the "crack" in the political system that can be exploited by the people disappears. Repression becomes a preferred option for local government when this method carries little risk while saving the cost of concessions. If repression is commonly used, it signals the risk of resistance in society. Although repression does not always deter protests, consistent repression likely reduces their numbers (Lichbach 1987).

The Chinese central government is suggested to have tolerated social protests for two primary reasons. One is that repressing nonpolitical protests damages regime legitimacy (O'Brien and Li 2007; Cai 2008a). The government has claimed that it is the people's servant, and the mass line (i.e., attending to the people's needs) is its ruling ideology (Chen 2012). The other reason is that the central government may see local protests as a source of information about grassroots society (Lorentzen 2013).

However, both reasons are soft constraints on the central government. For one, the Chinese central government has multiple sources of information and it does not have to rely on social protests for information. For another, when the central government feels the threat rising from social protests, regime legitimacy is no longer its top concern. When the central government signals its tolerance of repression to local governments, the political environment is not conducive to the mobilization of collective action. In the Chinese political hierarchy, because the local government commonly carries out repression, it is likely to shoulder more blame for the repression than the central government.

This Element explores how government coercion affects popular contention, particularly in the administration of Xi Jinping. Social protests began to decline in China during the Xi administration after a steady increase for about two decades. The decline can be attributed to a variety of factors, such as decreases in the sources of conflict, but the decline has also been accompanied by more frequent use of coercion. Since Xi came to power in late 2012, the Chinese central authority has time and again signaled its intolerance of dissident and rights-protection activities. Consequently, participants in collective actions were more likely to face sanctions than before. Large-scale collective actions have declined drastically in China in recent years. This Element does not conclude that coercion or repression is the only reason for the decline in social protests in China, but rather it demonstrates how political opportunity shaped by the central authority's preference affects local government behavior and thereby the occurrence of collective action.

Large-scale contentious actions are more threatening to the regime than small ones. In China, coercion is not the only reason for the lack of large-scale regime-threatening protests. Regime-challenging collective actions often require a large amount of participation (Kurzman 1996; Castells 2015). In China, in addition to coercion, several other factors have contributed to the lack of large-scale action.

First, citizens' grievances are often specific to particular groups or localities, or common grievances vary in severity across localities. Peasants and workers, for example, have not acted together even though they might both face economic difficulties (Bernstein and Lü 2003). This is because they believe that their problems were caused by different factors. There is also a lack of coordinated action even among those in the same social group. For instance, worker resistance in China takes the form of "cellular activism" (Lee 2007, 10), constituting pockets of action instead of coordinated actions.

Second, the government has tried to prevent the accumulation of grievances by responding to some groups of the aggrieved. This measure reduces the total size of the aggrieved. Third, fast economic growth over the past few decades has created a large number of beneficiaries who depend on and/or trust the regime. As the regime still enjoys high public trust (Chen 2004; Tang 2005; Wright 2010), the aggrieved may delink their daily-life grievances from the central authority or the political system, blaming local actors for their problems instead. Finally, propaganda and nationalism have been consistently used to help the regime shore up its legitimacy. Thus, regime stability in China is maintained because of coercion, legitimacy building, and blame avoidance on the part of the central government.

However, as long as government policies cause grievances, collective resistance remains possible. For this reason, the Chinese government has limited the opportunities for collective resistance. This Element contributes to the understanding of contentious politics in authoritarian regimes. First, literature on social movements stresses the importance of political opportunity, but it generally focuses on national governments. Or, it tends to focus on macrolevel changes that trigger social movements or social protests (e.g., Tarrow 1998; McAdam 1999). In the Chinese political system, the political opportunity for protests – at least those that do not directly challenge Chinese Communist Party (CCP) authority or the political system – is more closely tied to local politics, and macrolevel influence is exerted through the interaction between the central and local governments. The China case illustrates how the political system shapes local political opportunities for collective action.

Second, this Element sees central–local relations in China as a dynamic rather than static interaction. Some studies on contentious politics in China point out the various means that local authorities may use to deal with collective actions (Chen 2012; Lee and Zhang 2013). Others also explore the influence of the central government on local responses to such actions (Bernstein and Lü 2003; O'Brien and Li 2007; Cai 2010). Yet, existing studies on the interaction between the central and local governments tend to view the interaction as static, and a static relationship fails to capture the fluctuation in the magnitude of collective action in China. By contrast, a dynamic relationship sheds light on the expansion and contraction of political opportunities or the rise and fall of collective actions.

The remainder of this Element is organized as follows. Section 2 explains the challenges arising from social protests that authoritarian governments face, despite these governments' efforts to create an unorganized society. In Section 3, we discuss the various dispute-resolution measures and control mechanisms created by the Chinese government to deal with social conflict. In Section 4, we develop a framework that explains how collective action becomes possible or difficult given the political opportunity shaped by the interaction between the central and local authorities in China. Drawing on a collection of more than 10,000 cases, Section 5 provides an overview of collective actions in China from 2000 to 2017, showing that more collective actions have been staged by people working in the nonstate sector, and describes the distribution of social protests over the years. This section also discusses the participants' choice of targets in collective action.

Section 6 discusses the use of coercion in China. It explores the rise of a repressive social environment after Xi Jinping came to power and explains the government's use of coercion in ensuring social stability and how coercion shapes political opportunity in China. Section 7 discusses the relationship between social protests and social stability in China. It points out the government's efforts to prevent the accumulation of grievances and its measures to win support from the public. Many grievances are specific to certain localities or social groups in China, and focal issues that give rise to widespread grievances are limited. In addition, many people delink their grievances from the regime. This delinking combined with economic growth has created a large number of beneficiaries, subsequently lending support to the regime. The final section concludes by discussing government measures and social stability in China.

2 Protests as Challenges to Authoritarian Regimes

Authoritarian governments pay serious attention to social protests because protests create uncertainties. For one, even a strong authoritarian government is unable to prevent all collective actions. The government may be able to eliminate all formal organizations calling for collective action, but networks for mobilization may still exist in other forms. For another, the government faces uncertainty in dealing with social protests, and inept responses can escalate social protests into regime-toppling collective action (Goldstone and Tilly 2001). In China, the party-state has ensured regime stability by eliminating potential regime challengers and prohibiting independent social forces. However, the government is not immune to the uncertainties associated with social protests.

Ensuring Regime Stability in China

Authoritarian rulers need to exercise effective control over the ruled in order to prevent revolts from below (Svolik 2012). One fundamental solution to the challenge is to eliminate all possible challengers in society by applying coercion and repression. This has been the consistent policy adopted by the Chinese party-state. Soon after the CCP came to power in 1949, it began to consolidate power by repressing and purging those deemed as challengers to communist rule, or the so-called counterrevolutionaries. Those targeted included bandits, spies, local tyrants, supporters of the previous Kuomintang regime, counterrevolutionary activists, and leaders of religious organizations and social associations.

An estimated 2.6 million bandits were wiped out in these crackdowns (Bai 2009, 156). From 1949 to 1952, around 1.58 million counterrevolutionaries were repressed, with 873,600 sentenced to death (Ying 2011), in addition to those who committed suicide. An estimated two million people were executed as landlords during the land reform campaign after the CCP came to power (Teiwes 1987). Similarly, a large number of people in urban and rural China were purged during the Three- and Five-anti campaigns between 1951 and 1952, whereas others committed suicide.[3] In a 1958 speech to the police department, Luo Ruiqing, the Minister of Public Security, described the

---

[3] It was estimated that more than half a million people committed suicide during the suppression of counterrevolutionaries and another 200,000 during the Three- and Five-anti campaigns (Chow 1960, 115, 133).

purge policy that had been enforced from 1949. He claimed that this policy aimed to "resolutely, thoroughly, neatly, and comprehensively wipe out all antirevolutionaries. Our Party has explicitly and resolutely stuck to this correct policy regardless of the opposition of others" (Luo 1994, 408).

These repeated crackdowns on (perceived) regime challengers, together with rural collectivization and urban nationalization, served to dramatically change, if not eradicate, traditional social structure in Chinese society after 1949. The CCP began to establish its dominant presence in the country. Suppressing independent social organizations has remained a consistent policy in China; the regime is likely to crack down on social organizations that it perceives as a threat (Tong 2009). Chinese society has therefore become unorganized, in that intermediary organizations, including religious groups, are weak.

However, a lack of independent social forces does not guarantee regime stability, as evidenced by a series of social protests or movements mobilized by citizens throughout the history of Communist China. For example, there were waves of worker strikes in the 1950s (Perry 1994). The Cultural Revolution from 1966 to 1976 involved massive participation on the part of citizens, some of whom were not mobilized by the state. Factions in certain areas became so radical and violent that they necessitated repression by the military (e.g., Wang 1995). There have also been political actions or actions with political claims. In 1976, after Premier Zhou Enlai's death, a large number of people staged spontaneous popular demonstrations in Tiananmen Square, constituting a direct "challenge to the regime from below" (Teiwes and Sun 2004).

To date, the most severe direct challenge to Communist rule in China has been the 1989 Tiananmen movement. This movement was first initiated by students and was then sustained for about two months because of a split among national leaders, including Deng Xiaoping, CCP General Secretary Zhao Ziyang, and Premier Li Peng. This movement ended with the bloody crackdown on June 4, 1989, following the purge of Zhao (Zhang and Link 2001). The 1989 crisis suggests that even an unorganized society can mobilize protests when political opportunities arise. In the aftermath of the 1989 student movement, Deng Xiaoping stressed the importance of a united leadership. He said,

> The core issue of China is that the Chinese Communist Party has a good Politburo, especially a good standing committee of the Politburo. As long as the committee does not have a problem, China will be as steady as a rock (*wen ru taishan*) . . . The critical issue is the presence of a united core leadership. If we maintain such a leadership for 50 or 60 years, a socialist China will be invincible. (Deng 1993, 365)

However, a united leadership does not always ensure social stability in authoritarian regimes. Geddes et al. (2018, 179–180) show that more dictatorships fell to coups than to other kinds of challenge between 1946 and 2010. The second most common means of ending dictatorships were elections won by someone not supported by the dictatorship. Overthrow by popular uprising occurred less often before 1990, but has become much more frequent since the end of the Cold War. Mass protests remain a cause of regime collapse, as evidenced by the 2010–11 Jasmine Revolution in Tunisia and Egypt's revolution of 2011. Thus, uncertainties arising from social protests remain in authoritarian regimes, which prompts governments to be consistently risk conscious.

Mobilization in a Repressive Regime

The Chinese party-state has by and large prevented the emergence of independent organizations like trade unions that can orchestrate collective action against the will of the state. However, collective action in China is possible because of participants' moderate claims and the existence of mobilization networks. In his study on citizens' political participation in the former Soviet Union, Bialer (1986, 16) distinguishes "high politics" from "low politics." High politics refers to abstract political ideology, issues concerning the political system or national politics, or general social issues, whereas low politics refers to decisions directly affecting the daily lives of citizens, community affairs, and workplace conditions. He finds that the people of the Soviet Union generally lacked interest in high politics, but rather were concerned with low politics. This is also true for Chinese citizens who take action often not to challenge the political system or the Party's rule; instead, they take action to address their low-politics or nonpolitical issues.

In China, mobilization is still possible because of preexisting or newly established social networks among citizens (Pun 2007; Deng and O'Brien 2014; Luo and Andreas 2016; Zhou and Ai 2016; Lu and Tao 2017). Certainly, when recognizable organizations are involved in mobilization, they do not make political claims because of the risks this entails. Mobilization is possible also because prospective participants and activists strategically choose low-risk approaches (Fu 2018). In addition, citizens' reactive responses to unwelcome projects or developments often require minimum mobilization. For example, in a number of large-scale environmental protests in Chinese cities, residents were mobilized through new social media, despite their lack of preexisting networks (Huang and Yip 2012). When a large number of people become aggrieved, collective action is possible as long as some of the prospective participants have a consensus on the need for action or reach a critical mass, though mobilization can be further facilitated if preexisting networks exist (Calhoun 2013).

Protest leaders may still emerge in an unorganized society despite the risks, and even in a hostile political context, these leaders can adapt to the changing environment and coordinate collective action effectively (Kuang and Gobel 2013). In rural China, protest leaders may emerge from among capable residents through collective action. These leaders may be former government officials, incumbent or former village cadres, clan elders, schoolteachers, religious figures, and others with education or simply strong personalities. These leaders shape individually felt grievances into collective claims, recruit activists and mobilize the public, devise and orchestrate collective action, and organize cross-village actions (Li and O'Brien 2008; Wang 2012; Zhang, Wu 2015). Worker leaders similarly play an important role in framing contention and in choosing tactics from the repertoire of contention (Chen, Feng 2008).

In addition, mobilization networks can be created or strengthened after collective action starts. Some regime-toppling collective actions are not pre-planned or well organized, and opportunities for successful action can be created or expanded after the action starts (Kurzman 1996). The 1989 fall of Nicolae Ceauşescu, the ruler of Communist Romania, was not caused by organized action but by an unplanned uprising. Although soldiers were required to "sign a statement ... vowing we would support and protect Ceausescu" (Graham-Harrison 2014), the same military unit executed him after the mass protests occurred.

With the emergence of new ICTs, the possibility of mobilization increases (Bellin 2012; Castells 2015; Lei 2017). As Shirky (2011, 28) writes, "Social media have become coordinating tools for nearly all of the world's political movements, just as most of the world's authoritarian governments are trying to limit access to it." In addition, even a repressive regime may not prevent social protests because collective actions occur not only because of political oppor-tunity but also because of threat. Individuals tend to accept risk when they face losses (Scott 1976). Tilly (1978, 134–135) contends that "a given amount of threat tends to generate more collective action than the 'same' amount of opportunity." When citizens' rights are frequently violated or threatened, col-lective action remains an option.

Dynamic Process of Collective Action

Social protests threaten authoritarian rulers also because the dynamic process of collective action may produce unpredictable outcomes. In a repressive regime, social protests signal not only the grievances of society but also the limitations of the state's control, because the state would prefer such resistance not to occur and yet it does. The process is dynamic in that participants, bystanders, and the government toward which the action is directed keep updating their assessment of the prospects of the protest. This dynamic process influences the protest outcome by disclosing the weakness of the regime, reducing the risk of participation and creating a bandwagon effect among bystanders (Kuran 1991; Lohnmann 1994).

In authoritarian regimes, when the number of participants in a collective action increases, the larger number not only reveals the unpopularity of the regime or the preferences of a large population (Lohnmann 1994), but also the regime's weaknesses. As the number of participants increases, more people who are dissatisfied with the government are encouraged to participate. Bystanders may change their attitude toward the movement because their perception of risk is reduced or because they face pressure arising from nonparticipation (Kurzman 1996). The dynamic process can create or expand political opportunities for successful action, thereby encouraging more participation.

Thus, if social protests are not handled effectively in the initial stage, authoritarian rulers may face great uncertainty. Inconsistent policies or state vacillation between repression and concessions can only worsen the situation (Lichbach 1987). A split in the ruling elite is one dimension of political opportunity (Tarrow 1998), and such a split can be caused or expanded by ongoing protests. When mass protests escalate, the military may hesitate to follow the bidding of the government by suppressing the action. If the military refuses to open fire, the fate of the authoritarian regime is sealed. Likewise, if repression becomes ineffective or backfires (Abrahamian 1982, 515–516), regime collapse is likely.

The uncertainties arising from social protests prompt authoritarian rulers to take social protests seriously in order to prevent them from escalating into a challenge to the regime or from being taken advantage of by political rivals or opposition forces. The Chinese government is no exception, and it has prioritized social stability. In addition to instituting multiple measures of dispute resolution and social control, the Chinese central government has also contained collective action by shaping the political opportunities available to the aggrieved. In a political system consisting of multiple levels of government, the opportunity for collective action is determined by the interaction between the central and local authorities.

3 Conflict Management in China

China has been undergoing multiple great changes, including urbanization and marketization, that have caused a large amount of conflict in the past two decades.

These many conflicts and the possibility of their escalation have led the Chinese party-state to make maintaining social stability its top priority. Chinese central and local governments have created various dispute-resolution institutions to address social conflicts. Local governments are assigned the responsibility of maintaining local stability (Edin 2003; Whiting 2004). Their most common responses to social conflict include concessions or accommodation, repression, and ignoring the conflict. Chinese local governments do not always rely on coercion or repression for conflict resolution, and they sometimes make concessions to the aggrieved (Cai 2010; Lee and Zhang 2013). Yet, social control and monitoring have become routine practice for local governments, and coercion has remained crucial to silencing the aggrieved.

Institutions, Tactics, and Conflict Resolution

In the face of numerous incidents of social conflict, Chinese local governments have created, strengthened, and coordinated a large number of organizations for conflict resolution. These organizations include government agencies, legal departments, stability-preserving offices, and other civil organizations like the people's mediation committees. By 2017, China had 780,000 people's mediation committees, including 45,000 sector-specific and professional mediation committees (e.g., mediation committees for medical disputes). These mediation committees were staffed by 3.85 million people, with 14.2 percent of them being full-time mediators. These committees reportedly mediated about 9.02 million disputes in 2016 (Liu, Yizhan 2017).

These multiple channels initially remained loosely structured and less standardized, and the Chinese local state is not always a well-coordinated actor that can adopt consistent policies in dealing with societal forces (Fu 2017). Given rising social conflict, the government has strengthened local institutional realignment and integration of different dispute mechanisms, including legal institutions (Su and He 2010). Local governments commonly adopt a so-called grand mediation that relies on mediation but links various social and governmental resources together, with the aim of resolving conflict more effectively (Hu 2011). Grand mediation involves legal institutions or the courts, government agencies, and the people's mediation committees. The basic function of grand mediation is to "provide an alternative channel for ordinary people to pursue remedy rather than to appeal through collective actions so as to prevent the mass grievances from the grassroots level, which can minimize the potential challenges to the political order" (Ieong 2016, 97).

Coordinated action allows the government to solve and preempt more disputes at the grassroots level. The local state has developed strong mechanisms for case-by-case dispute resolution. Consequently, disputes are handled by different modes of settlement or by government agencies in coordinated and collaborative ways to secure quick and effective solutions and prevent them from escalating and spreading. This mode of conflict resolution has, in turn, strengthened the state's penetration into society (Chen and Kang 2016). Thus, "the Party-state's efficient, localized and mundane efforts in extending its reach to China's grassroots society have enabled the incumbent political regime to build its strength and consolidate the durability of its socio-political basis" (Yan 2016, 420).

Government involvement in dispute resolution does not necessarily solve citizens' grievances. Lee and Zhang (2013) suggest three microfoundations for Chinese local governments to maintain social stability: non-zero-sum bargaining, patron-clientelism, and legal-bureaucratic absorption. Non-zero-sum bargaining that involves the authorities spending money to "buy stability" is the most prevalent means of pacifying the aggrieved in labor, land rights, and property disputes. Such bargaining involves a combination of tactics, including efforts to soothe protesters' emotions, but also using or threatening to use force. The government has also tried to cultivate patron-client ties to help resolve social conflicts, often engaging CCP members, civil servants, the elderly and retirees, and former protest leaders as intermediaries.

Legal-bureaucratic absorption is a method of temporizing that saps the energy of the aggrieved and weakens their determination. As Lee and Zhang (2013, 1495) suggest, "the protracted and arduous processes of petition, arbitration, and litigation demobilize collective action by consuming aggrieved citizens' time, emotion, energy, and solidarity through endless rounds of red tape, paper chases, interminable waiting, and appeals." As a result, once conflicts enter the processes of petition, mediation, and litigation, officials can and do rely on the effects of bureaucratic procedures to buy time and reduce the visibility of unrest.

Such tactics can lead to two opposite outcomes. One is that lengthy bureaucratic procedures or a perfunctory response by state agents succeeds in weakening the will of disputants, and despairing people retreat into silence. However, ineffective bureaucratic procedures may alternatively drive people to escalate their action. For example, migrant workers' collective actions often have a legal basis, but their disputes are not necessarily solved via sanctioned channels because of the ineffectiveness of state bureaucracies or the legal system. As Lee (2007, 160–161) writes:

> The unpredictable and often corrupt bureaucracy and the legal system may ... add insult to injury and end up producing more frustration and

desperation than the initial workplace disputes did. Collective mobilization ... will overflow from the Labor Bureau and the court into the streets, and legal activism will be transformed into direct street action.

State offices at all levels receive petitions, ostensibly providing a means of redress for aggrieved citizens; yet evidence suggests that petitioning has limited effectiveness. Jilin is one of three northeastern provinces that have suffered from economic stagnation. Petitions in Jilin declined from over 500,000 in 2008 to 270,000 in 2010. During the three years from 2008 to 2010, a total number of 50,000 petitions reportedly brought about a solution to the source of the complaint (Peng and Guan 2011). If the number of petitions in 2009 in this province is assumed to be also 270,000, then the total number of petitions in Jilin from 2008 to 2010 exceeded one million. This implies, however, that only 5 percent of all petitions were addressed, and even this may overstate the success rate, as it relies on government-reported data. Whatever the exact figure, Chinese petitioners clearly face daunting odds.

Given the wide use of new ICTs, from 2013, the Chinese government began to promote "online petitions." In 2018, the National Complaints Bureau stated that five years after the online processing of petitions had been implemented, the number of online petitions had increased significantly across the country; its proportion of the total petitions kept increasing every year. During the first half of 2018, the number of online petitions processed by the National Complaints Bureau already accounted for more than 50 percent of all petitions (*People's Daily* 2018).

The government's reasoning is clear: If people use online petitions as a means to have their problems solved, they do not need to protest on the streets. However, if in-person petitions have limited effectiveness, there is no reason to believe that online petitions will be helpful either. Online petitioners generally receive a response from the system, but the response can be meaningless. Government responses to online grievances include refusing to respond, explaining policies, investigating a complaint, promising to address the problem, and solving a problem. It seems that many online complaints have not been solved.[4] Instead of using the official online petition system, some citizens report their problems on influential social media platforms to gain publicity. Cases that

---

[4] A scholar who conducted research on petitions in China reported that the statistics on online petitions released by state authorities are not necessarily accurate. Statistics on the results can be exaggerated. For example, the National Complaints Bureau forwarded about 1,000 online petition cases to authorities of one city in 2018, but fewer than thirty cases were solved. Yet, the local government reported a much higher percentage of resolved cases. In addition, some petitioners such as less educated peasants are less capable of presenting petitions online (private communication, July 2020).

gain high publicity are more likely to be solved (Cai and Zhou 2019), but most cases do not receive much public attention.

Chinese citizens who encounter injustices typically face a difficult situation when they seek redress. These people are often told or urged by the state authorities to use sanctioned channels to address their problems, but when these people resort to sanctioned channels by approaching pertinent agencies, it is not uncommon for them to fail to receive meaningful responses. In other words, if they use sanctioned channels, they are ignored, but if they resort to nonsanctioned means, they face constraints and risks because they can be accused of violating rules or the law.

Social Control in China

It is essentially impossible for the government to accommodate all of the aggrieved citizens in society. Threats, coercion, and repression remain crucial methods to ensure social stability in China. Chinese local governments achieve control and coercion through both institutional arrangements and government regulations. Such repression can be direct and indirect. This subsection discusses control mechanisms used by the Chinese government.

Organizational Control

The most important mechanism of direct organizational control in China is the work-unit system. Communist states commonly rely on organizational control to demobilize popular contention. Work-unit control is based on citizens' dependence on their workplace, which is controlled by the state. This dependence subjugates citizens to the state's control or commands their acceptance of the rules. In the former Soviet Union, the dependence of industrial workers on the state was crucial to maintaining labor peace. According to Linda Cook (1993, 2), "In exchange for such comprehensive state provision of economic and social security, Soviet workers consented to the party's extensive and monopolistic power, accepted state domination of the economy, and complied with authoritarian political norms. Maintenance of labor peace in this political system thus required relatively little use of overt coercion."

Similarly, Andrew Walder (1986) contends that in China before the 1980s, the work-unit system created workers' socioeconomic dependence on the enterprise, their political dependence on the management, and their personal dependence on their superiors. This pervasive pattern of "organized dependence" in factories effectively countered worker militancy. A similar political arrangement was created in rural China through collectivization (Oi 1989), and the commune system made the peasants depend on the collective for their livelihoods.

In the 1989 Tiananmen movement, a substantial number of people working in the state and public sectors took to the streets in Beijing and other cities to support the students, especially after the students began their hunger strike in Tiananmen Square on May 13, 1989. Therefore, work units or villages may facilitate collective action when there is solidarity among the members. Between May 15 and 19, more than 700 work units in Beijing had employees joining the movement. Most of these work units were state-owned units, including public firms, primary and secondary schools, universities, research institutes, news agencies, and state agencies. At least fifty national state agencies and twenty agencies of Beijing City had employees among the protesters (The Ministry of Education 1989, 121). When state employees took to the streets to protest against the state, they delegitimized the regime.

The participation of state employees in the Tiananmen movement motivated the central authorities to regulate public employees, prohibiting them from participating in collective action. In October 1989, the Law of the People's Republic of China on Assemblies, Processions, and Demonstrations prohibited state employees from initiating, organizing, or participating in social protests. In April 2005, the National People's Congress passed the Law of the People's Republic of China on Civil Servants. Article 53 decrees that civil servants are prohibited from spreading messages that damage the state's reputation, or from initiating, organizing, or participating in antistate assemblies, processions, demonstrations, or strikes.

The Chinese government has also regulated employees in public institutions (e.g., schools, research institutes, and public hospitals) that are (partly) funded by the government. In August 2012, the Ministry of Human Resources and Social Security promulgated the Interim Provisions on Disciplinary Actions against Staff Members of Public Institutions. Article 16 stipulates that employees of public institutions are proscribed from spreading messages that damage the national reputation, organizing or participating in collective action that harms national interests, or establishing or joining illegal organizations. Penalties include demerit, demotion, or dismissal from office. Thus, organizational control remains effective among those who work in the public sector in that disobedient employees face a credible threat from the party-state of losing their livelihoods.

However, socioeconomic changes since the late 1970s have drastically reduced the number of people who are subjected to the direct organizational control of the party-state. A socialist economy is characterized by the dominance of state ownership, but massive privatization and market reforms have greatly reduced the size of the public sector. The year 1998 represents the turning point: In that year, more people in cities began to work in nonstate units because of the dramatic reform of public firms. According to the National Bureau of Statistics of China (2016, 125), employees working in state-owned units declined from 56.7 percent to 15.4 percent of the working people in urban China between 1996 and 2015. By contrast, the self-employed and those working in the private sector accounted for 83.4 percent of urban employees by 2015.

These changes in the employment structure imply that the majority of disputes are no longer addressed within the work unit as before. Private as opposed to state employment does not increase collective action per se, but is more conducive to mobilization when conflicts and grievances arise. In the past two decades, socioeconomic changes, such as industrial restructuring, urbanization, and urban development, have given rise to numerous conflicts in China and episodes of collective action. Given the waning levers of traditional control based on the work unit and the former collective farming system, the Chinese government responded by strengthening, or creating new, institutions of monitoring and control.

New Means of Social Control

For decades, the Chinese party-state has bolstered its cross-unit or community-based institutions to monitor the population. In part, it has reformed and strengthened the networks of residents' committees that have blanketed the cities since the early years of the People's Republic of China (Read 2000, 2012; Wong and Poon 2005; Bray 2006). And more recently, local governments have commonly adopted the so-called grid-style or net management in local communities (Tang 2020). Specifically, the local government divides the locality under its jurisdiction into a number of small zones, with each zone monitored by a designated person. These designated people regularly report the situation in their respective zones to corresponding upper-level authorities. In the countryside, village cadres are recruited as the monitoring agents, whereas specialized personnel are recruited in cities (Cai 2019). The information provided by the grid managers is extensive, including various types of grievances of the residents.

The government has also strengthened its existing monitoring taskforce. Different levels of the stability-preservation offices extend great efforts to screen and detect social conflict (Yan 2016). In some places, the screening is conducted once a week at the village level and twice a week at the township level. Such activities include field investigation, information gathering and analysis, and household visits and discussions with pertinent parties. The Chinese government has instituted roadside patrols, 24-hour surveillance, and rapid-reaction forces in cities. In rural areas, police are assigned to monitor peasants, associations are formed for monitoring purposes, and volunteers are recruited for information collection (Chung 2012, 33–34).

Local governments have also extended the reach of the state to public spaces. Conflicts in urban China are contained within the gated structures of neighborhoods to prevent systemic challenges to the government. The penetration of the state is achieved not only through the organizational network but also through state discourses on the need to maintain social stability (Tomba 2015). The state has also strengthened its presence and influence in urban residential communities in other ways, including through grassroots NGOs in neighborhoods. The party-state has begun to establish primary party organizations outside traditional institutions to extend and maintain its presence. Various territories or spaces, such as office buildings and business districts, have become sites for party building. In this way, "the highly mobile new social strata in the non-state sector can be partially 'stabilized' in various territories/spaces through the organizational networks of the CCP" (Zhang, Han 2015, 662). In recent years, the party-state has also established cells in private businesses, including foreign companies, to increase its presence and control over society.

Monitoring Social Media

Social media have become an important tool for mobilizing collective actions, some of which can be threatening to authoritarian regimes. In the case of the 2010–11 Arab Spring in the Middle East, grievances alone could not explain the sudden surge in popular protest, either in terms of its timing or its location; the timing and swelling of the popular uprising in both Tunisia and Egypt came about via the combined role of social media and satellite television (Bellin 2012). Authoritarian governments now commonly exercise control or censorship to manage social media in order to limit their mobilization power.

New ICTs have also been used by Chinese citizens to mobilize collective action (Liu 2013). A series of large-scale environmental protests were orchestrated through social media, as discussed in Section 5. The Minister of Public Security acknowledged in 2005 that the development of ICTs, while facilitating social and economic development, has created serious pressures on maintaining social stability in China (The Editorial Group of Red Flag 2005, 102). The police department in Shenzhen acknowledges that protesting groups were not connected to one another in the past. However, protestors now pay more attention to coordinated action that involves a greater number of participants and is therefore more powerful. "Some websites and cellphone messages often become important mechanisms for coordinating actions. It is increasingly common for participants in collective action to use modern communication technologies and the Internet to spread information and draw public attention to their issues" (The Police Bureau of Shenzhen 2006, 19).

Precisely because of their effectiveness, the Chinese party-state has exerted great efforts and allocated a huge amount of manpower and resources to monitoring social media (Lei 2017). As early as 2013, China had about two million "analysts of online public opinion" who worked for the propaganda department, news portals, and internet companies (Tu and Xu 2013). These people searched websites and collected information for the government and internet companies. Social media can serve as a channel for the government to collect information about the public's reaction to certain issues. However, not all critical online messages trigger the same kind of reaction from state authorities. King, Pan, and Roberts (2013) suggest that messages indicating or instigating collective action are most likely to be censored, while the government may tolerate discussions or even criticisms of government policies. State agencies responsible for cyberspace management are guided by the following principle: "effective control [*guan de zhu*] is the imperative [*ying daoli*]" (*People's Liberation Army Daily* 2016). In 2016, the Chinese government enacted the Cybersecurity Law, which further empowers the government and the police in cyber management.

The government's monitoring creates a "common knowledge constraint" for people who mobilize collective action through social media (Cai and Zhou 2016). Specifically, the information about collective action disseminated to prospective participants by protest organizers can also be learned by the government. This information is common knowledge for both the participants and the government. With this knowledge, the government can make preparations to preempt the action or contain its impact. Thus, local governments and police departments constantly monitor social media to locate protest organizers and take preventive measures. Although the government cannot prevent all collective actions mobilized through new ICTs, it can preempt many large-scale ones that require more mobilization efforts.

State Sanctions

Authoritarian governments commonly use a wide range of coercive measures to deter or discipline defying behaviors. Steven Levitsky and Lucan Way (2010, 57–58) divide coercion in authoritarian regimes into two types: high-intensity coercion and low-intensity coercion. The former refers to high-visibility acts that target a large number of people, well-known individuals, or major institutions, whereas the latter refers to surveillance, low-profile (but not necessarily less severe) physical harassment, denial of employment, scholarships, university admission, and public services, and use of tax, regulatory, or other state agencies to investigate and prosecute those who oppose.

Many of these measures have been applied in contemporary China to ensure social stability (Wang and Minzner 2015). For example, the crackdowns on the 1989 Tiananmen movement and Falun Gong and the detention of well-known political dissidents (e.g., Liu Xiaobo, the Nobel prizewinner who died in 2017) are examples of high-visibility repression. Sanctions against defying citizens like petitioners and protestors can be divided into three categories: (1) legal charges; (2) extralegal measures; and (3) illegal measures. Legal sanctions are a common method. Almost all modes of collective action in China are illegal. Collective petitions are a common mode of collective action in China (Chen 2012), yet the number of participants in a collective petition may not exceed five. Strikes are outlawed by the Chinese Constitution, whereas demonstrations require the approval of the police department, which is almost impossible to obtain for most people. Although people who violate these regulations or the law are not necessarily disciplined, there exists the possibility. Criminal charges against participants in protests include violating laws against illegal gatherings or demonstrations; mobilizing the masses to storm state agencies; disrupting work order, public order, or traffic; mobilizing the masses to disrupt social order; organizing, leading, and participating in organized crimes; and subverting the government (Cai 2008b).

Extralegal measures include government agencies applying coercion to targeted individuals through "relational repression" (Deng and O'Brien 2013). Here, local officials investigate activists' social ties and locate individuals who might be willing to help stop the protest, such as protestors' relatives, friends, and neighbors.

Finally, given their political and administrative power, local governments may also resort to illegal means to punish disobedient citizens. For example, petitioners can be detained under false accusations. In Henan Province, a petitioner was put in a mental hospital from 2003 to 2009 when his repeated petitions upset local authorities (Luo, 2010). Another illegal means is hiring thugs who use violence or the threat of violence to intimidate recalcitrant citizens (Chen 2017; Ong 2018).

Chinese local governments are thereby empowered with a wide range of means to deal with disobedient citizens and handle social protests. Both accommodation and coercion are possible. Depending on local governments' resources and their perception of the risk of repression, they react differently to the actions of aggrieved citizens. As discussed in the next section, local responses are shaped by the interaction between central and local governments, and the interaction determines the political space available to the aggrieved who intend to stage resistance.

4 Opportunity for Collective Action in China

The Chinese political hierarchy consists of five levels of governments: the central authority; the provincial government; the municipal government; the county government; and the township government. The village authority is, in theory, not a level of government but a self-governance organization, but in reality it performs government duties. It is often the local governments at the county and municipal levels instead of the central government that directly deals with social disputes.[5] As discussed later, local governments have been most frequently targeted by aggrieved citizens either because the former have caused the grievances (i.e., they are the target of blame) or because they are believed to be able to solve the grievances (i.e., they are the target toward which people's action is directed).

While generally not handling social protests directly, the Chinese central government makes policies for and gives guidance to local governments to deal with social protests (Hess 2013). The central government's attitude toward the aggrieved shapes local government responses to local protests. Opportunities arise when the central government is less tolerant of the local government's use of repression, and opportunities diminish when the central government signals its tolerance of local repression. A repressed environment is created when the central government becomes repressive and the local government behaves accordingly.

Political Opportunity in China

The Chinese state is not a monolithic actor. For analytical convenience, this Element divides the state authority into central and local. Opportunities for collective action in China arise from two types of disparities within the political regime: horizontal and vertical. Horizontal disparities refer to the differences between state authorities at the same level, similar to what Kenneth Lieberthal and Michel Oksenberg (1988) term "fragmented authoritarianism." These differences create cracks or political space for Chinese citizens to exploit for the purpose of protecting or pursuing their interests, sometimes by seeking allies from within the state (Shi and Cai 2006).

---

[5] As discussed in Section 5, in 93 percent of the cases of collective action from 2000 to 2017, the participants complained about local actors.

Vertical differences refer to those between different levels of authority, especially between the local and the central authorities (Bernstein and Lü 2003; O'Brien and Li 2007; Cai 2008a). For example, when local officials harm farmers through unauthorized taxes and extractions, the aggrieved may take action by appeals to state law or government regulations issued by higher-level authorities that protect citizens' rights. Such "rightful resistance," according to Kevin O'Brien and Lianjiang Li (2007, 2), "employs the rhetoric and commitments of the powerful to curb the exercise of power, hinges on locating and exploiting divisions within the state, and relies on mobilizing support from the wider public." This illustrates one method citizens may use to exploit the disparities between the central and local governments. These vertical disparities are believed to be crucial to the occurrence and success of social protests in China (Cai 2010).

Two types of constraints may compel the central authorities to behave differently from local authorities in their management of social protests, thus creating cracks for collective action. One is the legitimacy constraint and the other is the information constraint. In a society where the government controls all political power and political resources, it also assumes all the responsibilities of governance. The concentration of power makes it difficult for the government to avoid blame (Weaver 1986). However, even an authoritarian government is strongly motivated to avoid blame and protect its legitimacy.

Authoritarian governments cannot always rely on coercion to deal with aggrieved citizens, not only because repression can backfire but also because it weakens the regime's legitimacy. Legitimacy refers to the regime's worthiness of being respected and accepted, or "legitimacy means respect-worthiness" (Balkin 2004, 486). A legitimate regime is one that makes it worthy of respect, so that people living in the regime have reasons to accept its rule.

Barbara Geddes (1999) contends that authoritarian governments need "some support and a good deal of acquiescence to remain in power." Legitimacy is conducive to authoritarian rule because it saves the cost of repression or governance, though such governments do not rely on popular votes to stay in power. Seweryn Bialer (1986, 183) writes that in the long run, "the legitimacy of the political regime helps absorb the tensions and instability and endure the scarcities, deprivations, frustrated aspirations, and shortcomings of the political order." A government with a low level of legitimacy faces difficulties surviving political crises when alternatives become available to the people, in which case a "revolutionary situation" arises (Tilly 1978, 190).

The central party-state advances claims to legitimacy in countless ways. Leaders like Deng Xiaoping (1993) asserted that the CCP survived the 1989 crisis because its reform policies had benefited the public. Over the years, the Chinese government has always claimed that it is the government of the people. The Xi Jinping administration has recently tried to appeal to the masses by articulating a policy of "common prosperity."

In China, the central authority represents the system more than local authorities do, and the former is more concerned with the regime's legitimacy and the Party's survival than the latter. Thus, the central authority is more tolerant of the citizens' nonpolitical or low-politics actions because repressing such actions damages its image (Cai 2008a). When the citizens believe in the center's willingness to accommodate their claims, they commonly adopt "rightful resistance" by citing a legitimate basis for pursuing their interests (O'Brien and Li 2007). Because local governments sometimes do make concessions to protestors (Lee and Zhang 2013; Elfstrom 2021), protests remain a viable and sometimes effective means of political participation.

The need to collect information about local grievances in the face of information constraints is another possible reason for the central authority to tolerate local protests. Authoritarian rulers encounter difficulties in collecting reliable information about local agents or the local situation. A lack of information flow also creates what Ronald Wintrobe (1998) calls a "dictator's dilemma" – the more the dictator's repressive apparatus stifles dissent and criticism, the less they know how much support they really have among the population. In authoritarian regimes, social protests can be a source of information for the central authority. Peter Lorentzen (2013, 152) contends that:

> Authoritarian governments have limited sources of information about either the actions of the officials at their lower levels or the discontent of their citizens. Permitting protests provides information about both, helping to limit corruption and to bring discontented communities out in the open rather than driving them underground.

In addition, by allowing the media to report certain incidents of social protest, the state can identify and address severe issues (Huang, Boranbay, and Huang 2019). It merits mentioning that this information constraint applies only to the central government, not the local government, which is relatively well informed about local residents' grievances.

The legitimacy and information constraints imply that the central authority does not always support local repression of social protests. However, existing research that highlights central–local disparities appears to assume that the central authority's preferences are static. In fact, both constraints faced by the central authority are soft ones, and they vary across time. Although communist regimes are motivated to shore up legitimacy by accommodating the aggrieved, they do not hesitate in applying coercion when they feel the threat from the population. Social protests may be a source of information for the central government, but the central government does not have to rely on this source for information. Indeed, the central government has multiple sources of information, especially in an era of new ICTs. Thus, the legitimacy and information constraints faced by the central authority vary in light of its changing priorities.

Central Government and Local Opportunity

The local government's response to social conflict is shaped by its perceptions of the cost of concession, the power of the aggrieved, and the nature of people's claims (Cai 2010; Li 2019; Elfstrom 2021). In other words, the local response is determined by two sets of factors: the costs of concessions and the risks associated with repression (henceforth risks of repression). For the local government, the costs of concessions take different forms. A common one is economic, and another is political, in that it often requires disciplining the people, including officials, deemed responsible for the grievances (Cai 2008a). Economic issues often require compensation. Some local authorities may be willing to "buy stability," but others may not. Local authorities sometimes refuse to make concessions because concessions may encourage more protests or more demands.

Repression or coercion remain options for the local authority to handle social protests, but the local authority faces constraints when applying repression to deal with people whose demands do not challenge the regime. In China, citizens may have concerns over certain broad issues like corruption, but what commonly motivates their action is grievances concerning low-politics issues such as economic welfare benefits. When the local authority's repression of such action causes severe casualties or media exposure, local agents face the strong possibility of being disciplined by the central or high-level authority. Or, if the local authority's repression is ineffective, collective action may escalate. In these circumstances, local agents are also likely to be disciplined.

For example, peasants in a village in Hebei Province had a dispute with the city government over a piece of land in 2005. Peasants occupied and guarded that piece of land because they believed that the government that intended to take away the land had failed to provide enough compensation. As a response, the government hired more than 300 thugs to attack the peasants guarding the land early one morning, killing six and wounding another forty-eight. After a villager posted footage of the attack online, the provincial government immediately investigated the case. In the end, the city party secretary was jailed for life, and dozens of others were given legal penalties, including the death penalty (Cai 2010, 120–121).

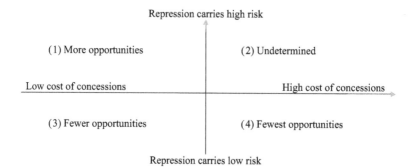

Figure 1 Risks and costs faced by local authorities determine political opportunities for collective action

Thus, as long as the Chinese central government hopes to project an image of itself as a "good emperor," local officials face risks when using repression. By the same token, local officials would not face serious penalties if their repression does not cause severe consequences. In other words, if the local authorities believe that the risks of repression are small, repression becomes an option that saves them the cost of making concessions.

Figure 1 presents a simplified illustration of the local authority's response to social protests or political opportunity for collective action. When the local authority faces low costs of concessions and high risk of repression, the local authority is more likely to tolerate collective action (i.e., Scenario 1). In other words, there will be more opportunities when the central authority is tolerant of collective action, in which case the risk of repression is high for the local authority. If the cost of concession is high and the risk of repression is low, the local government is more likely to use repression. Alternatively, if the central government becomes repressive, the local government will behave accordingly. In these circumstances, the citizens face great risk when staging collective action, and consequently, the political opportunity decreases (i.e., Scenario 4).

For example, in the 1990s, when the central government saw Falun Gong as a political threat, it decided to wipe the sect out. The central government formed a leading agency to coordinate the nationwide crackdown. Given the central government's priority of the suppression, local governments followed its bidding and made great efforts to repress this organization (Tong 2009). As a result, the political space for this sect no longer exists.

Thus, the central government's attitude toward the aggrieved affects local government behavior. When repression carries little risk for the local government or is even encouraged, opportunities for action by the aggrieved decrease.

In these circumstances, even if the cost of concession is low, the local authority may still opt for coercion because the cost of repression is even lower (i.e., Scenarios 3 and 4). If repression is widely and constantly used, the people will realize that it is the central government's policy. This belief discourages collective action. As Mark Lichbach (1987) finds, although repression does not always deter collective action, consistent repression tends to reduce it.

The central authority might become repressive for different reasons. One is that it prioritizes social control over legitimacy building. The CCP has claimed it is upholding the so-called mass line, or serving the people (Chen 2012). If it represses citizens who have legitimate claims, it damages its own image. This occurs either because the central authority feels an increased threat of social unrest or because political leaders aim to prevent political rivals from taking advantage of social unrest. The crackdown on the Tiananmen movement in 1989 signaled the Party's determination to ensure its political rule. It repressed Falun Gong because the sect was perceived as a political threat.

The central authority uses repression also because it believes in its effectiveness. Authoritarian rulers commonly rely on repression to deter defiant activities, including social protests (Levitsky and Way 2010, 57–58). Government sanctions (bans, arrests, executions, and martial law) undermine the ability of groups to mobilize resources (people, money, guns, and ideas) and challenge the government (Oberschall 1973; Tilly 1978). The deterrent effect of repression lies in that the terror "is also the memory and the threat, even the implied threat, that under certain circumstances it could return" (Ekiert 1996, 101).

Finally, the central government opts for repression also when it lacks resources to accommodate the aggrieved. During economic downturns, for example, the government may allocate more of its limited resources to the coercive state apparatus to ensure regime stability instead of distributing resources to the large aggrieved population. As discussed later, the Chinese government has used coercion to deal with people who lost their investments because the government did not want to accommodate these investors with its own resources.

The changing priorities of the central government directly affect the political space for collective action in China. Since Xi Jinping came to power at the end of 2012, the central government seems to be less tolerant of defiant activities in society, regardless of the causes of the grievances. When Xi first assumed power, he faced a series of challenges from the Party and society. In the Jiang Zemin and Hu Jintao administrations, rapid economic growth created a large number of beneficiaries, but some problems had also remained or worsened. Within the administrative system, local governments were believed to be unwilling to enforce certain policies made by the central government.

That "central policies are ignored outside Zhongnanhai" was said to be a feature of Hu Jintao's administration (Deng 2014). Corruption remained rampant and pervasive, whereas income inequality kept worsening. Most importantly, Xi's power base was far from strong when he first came to power.

Against this background, as discussed in Section 6, Xi's top priority was to consolidate power and that necessitated a stable political and social environment. Consequently, coercion was more commonly used than before. Time and again, the central government signaled its tolerance of local repression by making repressive policies or coordinating repressive moves. The more frequent use of coercion by local governments was directly associated with the decline in social protests in the country.

5 Social Protests in China

A large number of incidents of collective action have occurred in China in the past three decades, and these actions take on several features. First, they have become a mode of political participation by people across almost all social groups, ranging from peasants to workers, homeowners, and veterans. The commonplace nature of this mode of political participation suggests that existing laws and rules often fail to protect citizens' rights from being violated in the first place. And it reveals the limited effectiveness of sanctioned channels of dispute resolution, such as petitioning, as discussed in Section 3. Thus, collective actions are mostly reactive or defensive.

Second, collective action in China focuses mostly on low-politics issues concerning people's daily lives instead of demands for political rights. Protesting groups, such as workers, peasants, homeowners, taxi drivers, and veterans, all focus on tangible material interests when they stage action. This is an important reason that social protests do not constitute political challenges to the communist rule (Walder 2009). Given their nonpolitical claims, some of these protests are tolerated by the government. This Element does not focus on political actions, not only because political actions by dissidents – those who seek systemic change – are relatively uncommon in China, but also because the government response to such actions is straightforward intolerance, as in the case of Falun Gong (Section 4).

Third, local governments have become common targets of collective action. This is because local governments either caused the grievances or because they were believed to be better able to solve grievances that had been caused by other actors like lower-level governments or businesses. Our data also show that although there have been large-scale collective actions (involving more than 1,000 people), the majority of them are small. While social protests have persisted in China, the rising trend came to a halt after Xi came to power. Collective actions, especially large-scale ones, have declined drastically in recent years.

Data for This Study

Systematic data on social protests in China in the past few decades are lacking.[6] The number of publicly reported incidents of collective action in China rose from 8,700 in 1993 to about 127,500 in 2008,[7] but sanctioned sources stopped releasing aggregated statistics after 2008 (Chung 2012, 29). Research on social protests in China is often based on a small number of cases, but with notable exceptions. Yao Li's research (2019) on collective action in China is based on 1,418 cases that occurred from 2001 to 2012. Her study sheds important light on how protests are managed in China. Yet, the number of cases included in her research is relatively small compared with the large number of incidents that occurred during this period. In addition, the data do not include cases that occurred after 2012.

Han Zhang and Jennifer Pan constructed a data set of 100,000 cases of collective action collected from Sina Weibo. This is by far the largest data set on collective action in China, and it provides a solid foundation for an assessment of the magnitude of incidents of collective action, the types of grievances, and groups of participants in China. Yet, this data set only includes incidents that occurred from 2010 to 2017 (Zhang and Pan 2019), and thus it cannot be used to examine social protests before 2010. Another data set is based on a project called "Wickedonna" that collected over 74,420 cases from Chinese social media posts during a period of three years from July 2013 until June 2016. Using this data set, Christian Göbel (2021) explores the rationale behind government repression. He finds that repression is closely correlated both with the cost of concessions for local governments and protest intensity. However, despite its large size, this data set covers a short time span and contains limited information on reported cases. Thus, although these large data sets are valuable sources, they are insufficient in assessing trends in social protests in China.

The data used in this Element are drawn from our collection of more than 11,800 protest news events that occurred in China from 2000 to 2017.[8] Since 2007, our research assistants have been collecting news stories on social protests from fifteen online sources, including newspaper databases, six of

---

[6] A new method of case collection is online data mining. See Zhang and Pan (2019).
[7] These incidents are termed *quntixing shijian* (群体性事件 or mass actions) in the Chinese media.
[8] The data included in this study stopped in 2017 because the research team ran out of funding.

which are located outside of mainland China.[9] For a protest event to be included in the database, four criteria had to be met: it had to involve more than ten participants; it had to present either a grievance against some target or a demand made to some institution; it had to assume confrontational form; and it had to be located in the public sphere. Based on these criteria, nonconfrontational events, such as complaints, letter-writing campaigns, lawsuits, and press conferences, have been excluded. Petitioning (*shangfang*) events are included only if they escalated into public protests (e.g., holding demonstrations or sit-ins in front of government offices); legal and routine petitioning activities are not included in our database.[10]

Assessing whether the cases we collected are representative of the overall protest landscape in China is difficult. Relying on media reports may introduce bias into the data (Earl et al. 2004). First, for news reports in contemporary China, fluctuation in the number of protests over the years may be caused by the business operations of the news media or the degree of censorship. Hence, the number of reported protests may not accurately reflect the actual number of protests that have occurred. Second, protests by some groups (e.g., urban workers) may be more likely to gain media attention than others (e.g., peasants in remote areas). Small-scale protests are also less likely to be reported than large-scale ones. Therefore, certain kinds of protests may be underrepresented in the database. These possibilities certainly exist, but they do not necessarily invalidate the analysis in this Element as we have been carefully maintaining the validity and reliability of the database.

During data collection, the data sources have not been altered, and cases were systematically drawn from newspaper databases and news agencies. Furthermore, protest news published on blogs, new social media, or other online sources were not included in order to prevent the introduction of another layer of bias. Second,

---

[9] The cases were collected from a news database, Wisers (http://wisenews.wisers.net/wisenews) and three online news agencies. Wisers' news database provides full-text content from nine news agencies or newspapers published in China and two newspapers in Hong Kong, including中国新闻社 (China News Service), 新京报 (*The Beijing News*), 南方日报 (*Nanfang Daily*), 南方周末 (*Southern Weekly*), 南方都市报 (*Southern Metropolis Daily*), 华西都市报 (*Huaxi Metropolis Daily*), 广州日报 (*Guangzhou Daily*), 深圳晚报 (*Shenzhen Evening News*), 兰州晨报 (*Lanzhou Morning News*), 苹果日报 (*Apple Daily*), and 明报 (*Ming Pao*). The three online news agencies were Radio Free Asia, 博讯 (Boxun), and大纪元 (the Epoch Times).

[10] The reports that met these criteria were then coded for content. In collecting and coding the data, the procedures were subject to intensive reliability and validity checks. First, two coders were responsible for coding the same variables for each event. Then, their coded values for the variable were checked to see if they were a match. When two coded values of a variable for an event differed, a supervisor would check and decide on the correct value. We calculated the intercoder reliability by calculating the percent agreement for two coders when every one hundred values were coded for each variable. In general, above 90 percent was considered acceptable. If a result was lower than 90 percent, we would further examine the causes and clarify the coding procedures or subject the coders to more training sessions.

our data set includes about 2,415 large-scale protests, with 1,000 or more participants each. As large-scale protests are less likely to be covered up, they can be especially indicative of the Chinese government's protest management. Another study on protest events in China drawing on data from social and news media also finds that reporting bias in the news media is substantially reduced for large events.[11]

The China Labor Bulletin has also kept a record of worker protests in China since 2011. Its website reports 355 large-scale labor protests from 2011 and 2017. In contrast, our data include 1,546 cases of large-scale protests by various social groups during this period of time, or 4.4 times the figure reported by the China Labor Bulletin.[12] Our data include a greater variety of social groups than the collection of the China Labor Bulletin, which focuses more on urban employees.

In our collection, the list of variables includes characteristics of the protest event, including date, location, claims (the issue at stake), initiating social group, blame target, protest target, forms (tactics), number of participants, frequency, duration, and police response. In total, we registered 162 groups, including various occupational groups, status groups, and occasional groups.[13] These 162 groups were further consolidated into ten more general groups, including public-sector employees, private-sector workers, foreign-firm workers, veterans, urban residents (e.g., homeowners, displaced residents, and investors), religious and minority groups, petitioners, students, ad hoc groups, and peasants.

Grievances and Distribution of Protestors

Table 1 presents a total of 11,830 cases of social protests during different administrations: 2000–2 (the end of the Jiang Zemin administration); 2003–7 (the first term of Hu Jintao); 2008–12 (the second term of Hu Jintao); and 2013–17 (the first term of Xi Jinping). These cases suggest that, at least until recently, social protests have kept occurring in China, despite the government's efforts to maintain stability. Our data on the period between 2000 and 2002 is very limited because it only covers three years. But the data can serve as a reference

---

[11] Christian Göbel and Christoph Steinhardt. 2019. "Better Coverage, Less Bias: Using Social Media to Measure Protest in Authoritarian Regimes," Department of East Asian Studies, University of Vienna (unpublished manuscript).

[12] See the website of the China Labor Bulletin, http://maps.clb.org.hk/strikes/zh-cn.

[13] These are different types of groups of people. Each type of group includes a number of individual groups. For a protest event, by definition, there is one type of group (e.g., peasants, foreign-company workers, Tibetans, etc.). For example, the data have 10,000 cases, and these 10,000 individual groups are coded into 162 types of group.

Table 1 Distribution of protests in China (2000–17)

	2000–2	2003–7	2008–12	2013–17	Total
Public-sector employees (%)	30.8	18	13.3	7.4	10.9
Public employees (%)	3.5	5.2	7.2	4.4	5.3
Public firm workers (%)	27.3	12.8	6.1	3	5.6
Private-sector employees (%)	17.0	24.0	25.4	23.1	23.7
Urban residents (%)	19.7	24.1	29.7	36.8	32.9
Ad hoc groups (%)	5.9	7.8	7.9	5.9	6.7
Religious and ethnic groups (%)	5.9	1.1	4	2.1	2.7
Peasants (%)	20.8	25	19.8	24.6	23.1
Total protests	289	1,338	3,488	6,715	11,830
Percentage of total cases	2.4	11.3	29.5	56.8	
Large protests	103	366	781	1,165	2,415
Percentage of total cases	4.3	15.2	32.3	48.2	

Source: authors' collection

because public sources that include comparable information during the earlier years of the Jiang administration are unavailable.

It is obvious that collective actions have become a mode of political participation for a variety of social groups in China (Chen 2009; Chen 2020a). Protest participants can be divided into the following categories: (1) employees in the public sector; (2) employees in the private sector; (3) urban residents; (4) ad hoc groups or groups of people with mixed backgrounds; (5) peasants; and (6) other groups, such as ethnic minorities. Public-sector employees include civil servants, police, city management, medical staff, public schoolteachers, journalists, and other people working in the nonadministrative public agencies. Employees in public firms include those who work in state-owned enterprises or in urban collective firms.

Urban residents refer to those who come from the same group or have a similar status, including homeowners, students, and veterans. Ad hoc groups consist of protest participants previously unassociated with one another, who join protests because of issues of common concern (e.g., environmental pollution) or as participants in riots.

Labor disputes have been an important source of social conflict in China. In the early 2000s, workers from public firms protested most frequently because of industrial restructuring that mainly took the form of privatization, bankruptcy, closure, or reorganization. This reform resulted in massive layoffs, and widespread grievances among the laid-off workers and unpaid pensioners, because China had not established a fully encompassing welfare system or pension system at that time. Consequently, workers protested for layoff compensation, pension payment, medical care, and other economic issues (Hurst and O'Brien 2002; Lee 2007; Hurst 2009).

Our collection includes a large number of worker protests. It was common for workers in northeastern cities to block office compounds in the late 1990s and early 2000s, demanding salaries, severance pay, compensation, or pensions. Some workers also protested against their management. For example, in February 2000, tens of thousands of mine workers and their family members protested against low severance pay after their mine was declared bankrupt. In another case that occurred in Xi'an in September 2004, thousands of workers and retired workers blocked traffic, demanding that the factory that they worked for pay their salaries and medical expenditures. Workers were frustrated and angered because they had only been paid half of their salaries since February 2004. Protestors claimed that "old people need to eat," "children need to go to school," and "we need work." These protestors generally focused on welfare benefits instead of political rights, such as the right to organize themselves. With the completion of industrial restructuring after the early 2000s, protests by former employees of public firms began to decline drastically.

In contrast, protests staged by employees from the private sector accounted for a much larger portion of the total protests staged by urban employees from 2003 to 2017. According to the *Chinese Labor Statistical Yearbook* (1997–2017), the number of labor disputes accepted by labor management agencies rose from 48,121 in 1996 to 828,410 in 2016, increasing by 17.2 times. Of these cases, disputes over salary payment account for 47.4 percent, followed by disputes arising from the ending of labor contracts (26.3 percent), disputes related to social insurance (24.8 percent), and other disputes. The majority of these disputes occurred in the private sector, especially in Guangdong Province, which had the highest number of migrant workers in China (Lee 2007; Chan and Pun 2009). Workers protested over various welfare issues, such as salary nonpayment, payment delays, severance pay, compensation for work injuries, contract issues, and insurance, among others.

For example, in March 2014, 6,000 workers from a shoe factory in Shenzhen reportedly staged a demonstration, blaming the factory for cutting their pay from 4,500 yuan to 2,500 yuan per month. On March 10, workers gathered outside the factory, protesting against termination of employment without compensation. Workers were then dispersed by the police, who beat and arrested some of the participants. In December 2014, around 2,500 workers from another shoe factory in Panyu District in Guangzhou held a strike, protesting over issues related to labor contracts and social insurance premiums.

Urban residents were the group that staged the most collective actions from 2003 to 2017. This category of people protested over a number of issues that affected their tangible interests. A major source of conflict in urban China has been disputes between urban residents and local governments, developers, and property management companies over land use and housing demolition. Homeowners also have multiple complaints about community governance, including: a developer's failure to honor its promises; poor-quality housing; poor service from a property management company; occupying of public space by a developer or property management company; and manipulation of elections for homeowners' committees by a developer, a property management company, or the local government (Sheng 2019, 48).

Another cause for urban protests concerns environmental grievances. Environmental issues have sparked a series of large-scale protests in Chinese cities over the past two decades (Xie and van der Heijden 2010). Urban residents strongly oppose the construction or operation of chemical plants, fearing pollution. There have been influential cases in which large numbers of urban residents took to the streets in cities to protest against such projects.

A well-known case is one that occurred in Xiamen in 2007 when over 10,000 residents protested against a chemical project (Huang and Yip 2012). That year, a Taiwanese company obtained approval from the central and local governments to construct a chemical plant. But the project worried local residents, who then strongly opposed its construction. They relied on the Internet and cell phones to frame the issue and to orchestrate collective action by disseminating the place and time of protest. On May 28, a message entitled "Anti-pollution: A Million Citizens Spread the Word through SMS Like Crazy" was posted on a website whose server was located in Guangdong Province. The message stated that the chemical project would cause great damage to the environment and to people's health in the city, spurring many recipients to join demonstrations. On June 1, people from across Xiamen went to the city government, and the number of participants was estimated to exceed 10,000 at its peak. The following day, the number was smaller, but still in the thousands. The demonstrations put serious pressure on the city government, which eventually decided to suspend the project. Similar protests against chemical plants also occurred in other cities, often using ICTs as a major means of mobilization. These cities include Chengdu, Ningbo, Kunming, and Dalian (Cai and Zhou 2016).

Protests by peasants accounted for 20–25 percent of the total in our collection. Their large-scale protests accounted for 21 percent of the total (506 out of 2,415). As large-scale protests are less likely to be covered up, we believe that peasant protests may not be significantly underrepresented in our data.[14] Chinese peasants have protested for several major reasons. One is financial burdens before 2004, when the agricultural tax began to be abolished (Bernstein and Lü 2003; O'Brien and Li 2007). Heavy taxes and fees imposed by local authorities on peasants caused numerous incidents of social unrest in rural China before the early 2000s. There have also been deadly confrontations between peasants and local cadres. From 1992 to 2004, at least a hundred peasants died in violence related to tax collection (Cai 2010, 77).

A second reason is disputes over land use, which has remained one of the most important causes of rural protests since the early 2000s. When local authorities or state-supported businesses take away land from peasants without adequate compensation, conflicts between peasants and land users escalate into collective action (Chen 2020b; Zweig 2000; Guo 2001). One of the largest social protests organized by citizens in Communist China is the one that occurred in Hanyuan County in Sichuan Province in 2005 due to a dispute over land compensation (Shi 2005). In this case, the construction of a reservoir affected a large number of residents who believed that they had been under-compensated for the loss of their land and/or homes. According to reports, 100,000 people consequently staged a demonstration that turned into a riot in which a policeman was killed. As a result, twenty-eight participants were found guilty in court, one of whom was executed for killing the policeman.

A third major cause is pollution, which has also become a major source of grievances among rural residents who live near polluting factories (Deng and Yang 2013). There were about 350 "cancer villages" in China by 2013, most of them caused by polluting chemical materials (Gong and Zhang 2013). Not surprisingly, there have been protests against polluting projects in rural China. For example, peasants in Shanwei City in Guangdong protested against the construction of an electricity plant for fear of pollution in 2005. The protest was bloodily repressed, with three peasants shot dead and another eight injured.[15]

Map 1 presents the distribution of the number of social protests per million people across provinces and provincial level municipalities between 2000 and 2017. Guangdong, Hubei, Shaanxi, and Qinghai saw more protests than others. The three provinces in the northeast were well known for worker protests in the 1990s and early 2000s, though our collection only covers incidents that occurred after 2000.

---

[14] The relatively small number of protests in rural China may also have to do with urbanization and the shrinking population of villagers. According to the National Bureau of Statistics (2016, 85), the rural population decreased from 808.37 million in 2000 to 603.46 million in 2015, or by 25.3 percent.

[15] Other sources suggest a large death toll (French 2005).

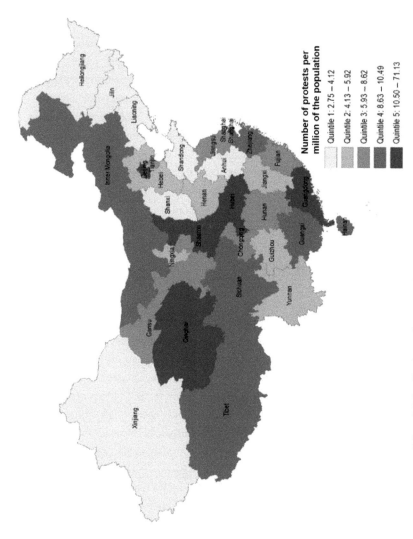

Map 1 Distribution of protests in China (2000–17) (per million people)

Number of protests per
million of the population

Quintile 1: 2.75 – 4.12
Quintile 2: 4.13 – 5.92
Quintile 3: 5.93 – 8.62
Quintile 4: 8.63 – 10.49
Quintile 5: 10.50 – 71.13

State Control and Mobilization

Despite authoritarian rule in China, mobilization of collective action is still possible. In addition to the rise of temporary protest leaders and the preexisting social networks discussed earlier, changes in the employment structure have also affected mobilization. Large-scale collective actions often involve some degree of mobilization or coordination, and their occurrence sheds light on the possibility of mobilizing collective action in China.

Our collection includes 2,415 large-scale protests whose participants can be categorized into three broad groups: (1) people from the same work unit; (2) people who share similar identities but come from different work units; and (3) people from different backgrounds and work units. The first group includes people in both public and private sectors. The second comprises people who share the same concerns but come from different work units or villages, such as home-owners who have staged collective actions to defend their interests. These people come from different backgrounds, but they share the same concerns over issues concerning their neighborhood. Another example is veterans who come from different places but fight for the same demands. The third group comprises people with different identities, work units, and backgrounds. These people protest over issues of common concern, such as environmental pollution. People from the same work unit staged 37 percent of the large protests, those with the same identity but from different work units staged approximately 49 percent, and those with mixed backgrounds staged less than 14 percent (Table 2).

These large-scale protests reveal multiple factors that contribute to mobilization in China. First, people from the same work unit can mobilize themselves because of the preexisting connections between them. In other words, the work-unit system

Table 2 Distribution of large-scale protests (2000–17)

Protestors' background	Cases	Frequency (%)	Presence of violence (%)
From the same unit	900	37.3	31.3
Public institutes	66	2.7	22.7
Public firms	213	8.8	28.2
Private firms	621	25.7	33.3
With the same identity	1,187	49.2	49.6
Urban residents	681	28.2	39.4
Peasants	506	21	63.4
Mixed backgrounds	328	13.6	66.5
Total	2,415	100	45.1

Source: authors' collection

may indeed contribute to the mobilization of collective action in certain circumstances. With the presence of such networks, large-scale protests may occur due to the high stakes for the participants. When people stand to lose if they fail to take action, collective action becomes possible. For example, in a city in Jilin Province in July 2009, the privatization of a state-owned steel factory triggered a riot wherein thousands of workers surrounded the office of the general manager, took him hostage, and beat him to death. Workers protested because of a rumor that a majority of them would be terminated after ownership reform. They took precipitous action because the stakes were high.

Second, new technologies and residential proximity contribute to mobilization. Among the 900 protests by people from the same work unit, nearly 69 percent were staged by employees from private firms. Mobilization of workers may not require great effort because emails, cell phones, or other online platforms can be used to disseminate information and coordinate collective action (Huang and Yip 2012; Liu 2013). New ICTs proved to be crucial in mobilizing people who were not previously connected, as discussed earlier.

Living together in dormitories provided by employers also creates an interactive environment conducive to workers' mobilization (Pun 2007). Countermobilization or demobilization by the management or the government becomes difficult when workers' mobilization is discreet or the threat from management is not credible.

Third, the state has not been able to exercise direct control over many participants. In our data, people with the same identity staged the most large-scale protests. These people often come from different backgrounds and are not subjected to the direct organizational control or reach of the government. For one, many of these participants did not work in state-owned work units or they were self-employed. For another, their protests might not be related to their work units, and they were less vulnerable to organizational controls. Homeowners, taxi drivers, and veterans have staged numerous protests in China, and their mobilization can be discreet and difficult to stop. As formal organizations are generally absent in collective actions against the will of the state, networks and solidarity among prospective participants have been crucial to the mobilization of collective action of almost all social groups in China.

Peasants staged 506 large-scale protests (or 21 percent). As discussed earlier, the state's control in rural society has been relaxed since the dismantling of the commune system. Village cadres further lost authority after the abolition of the agricultural tax. Although the government has strengthened its monitoring over rural residents (Yan 2016), protests have persisted. If a rural protest involves 1,000 or more participants, it is likely to include peasants from different villages.[16] These participants are not subjected to the control of any single village authority.

The government encounters challenges in demobilizing protests by people from different work units or backgrounds. Such people form temporary protesting groups that disappear soon after protests. As such protests are generally not organized by identifiable individuals, the government encounters a situation wherein "there is no organization to be banned" and "no conspiratorial leaders to round up or buy off" (Scott 1989).

The occurrence of violence seems to reflect the degree of the state's direct control over participants. Violence is more likely to occur in protests staged by people from different work units or backgrounds because these people are generally not subjected to the direct control of any authority during protests and they may feel little sense of risk. In contrast, protestors from the same organization, such as public agencies, are less likely to engage in violent protests (Cai 2010, 141–144). Participants from the same work unit or community can be tracked down more easily by the government than participants from different backgrounds; the former are therefore more risk averse and less inclined to use violence than the latter.

According to our collection, 1,089 of the 2,415 cases (or 45.1 percent) involved violence. The last column in Table 2 presents the occurrence of violence in protests staged by different groups. Peasants seemed to be more likely to use violence than other groups of people. One reason was that land disputes have been a major cause of peasants' protests, and peasants often used violence in such disputes in response to violence on the part of those encroaching on their land (Cai 2010, 146–147). People with mixed backgrounds used violence more frequently (in 66.5 percent of cases); people from the public sector (22.7 percent) or public firms (28.2 percent) used violence less frequently.

Upward Targeting

Chinese protestors have two targets of their action: the target of blame and the target of action. The former refers to those who are blamed for causing the grievances, whereas the latter refers to those who are approached by the aggrieved for solutions to their problems. These two targets may or may not overlap. Our collection of 11,025 cases contains information on both targets, revealing two patterns. One is that governments at all levels remain the major target of blame. In about 57 percent of the cases (Figure 2), protestors blamed

---

[16] In China in 2008, there were 703.99 million total people living in 604,000 administrative villages. On average, each village had 1,165 people. Excluding children, aged villagers, and those working outside villages, this means that there would be fewer than 1,000 who are able to participate in protests (The Statistical Bureau 2010, 5).

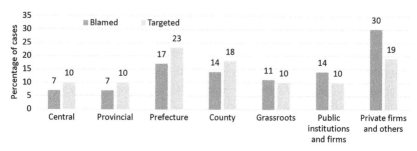

Figure 2 Targets of blame and action (percent of cases)
Source: authors' collection

one or another level of government, from central to village, whereas 43 percent of the protests blamed firms and other actors. However, among the targets of action, governments account for 72 percent, whereas nongovernment actors account for 28 percent. In other words, in about 15 percent of the cases, protestors focused their efforts on the government even though they did not blame the government for causing their grievances.

There is thus a phenomenon of "upward targeting" among Chinese citizens in the sense that they tend to approach state authorities or upper-level governments to have their problems addressed (Chen and Cai 2021). Upward targeting occurs because the government monopolizes political power and is believed to shoulder broad responsibilities. This explains why people who face civil disputes also approach the government. For example, in one city, among the 484 repeated collective petitions received by the government between 2010 and 2014, about 51 percent were caused by civil disputes (Xia 2019). Another reason for upward targeting is that protestors seek to enlist the backing of higher-level authorities against local officials. By approaching a higher level of government, protestors expected it to exert pressure on its subordinates who would then respond to the protestors.

For example, a traffic accident occurred in Jiangxi Province in May 2011, in which a motorcyclist from Town A ran into two individuals from Town B, killing one and injuring the other. The driver was too poor to pay the 200,000 yuan in compensation demanded by the victims' families. The two families then carried the body and staged a protest in front of the government of Town A. The county government went to mediate, but to no effect. In the end, the city leaders intervened and required each of the two town governments to pay 50,000 yuan to the two families; the driver borrowed a further 100,000 yuan to pay the families (Chen, Baifeng 2013). These cases indeed confirm people's belief in the effectiveness of seeking government intervention when they have disputes.

However, upward targeting is generally localized in China, in that local governments handle the most protests. Of those targeting governments, 10 percent targeted the central government while 61 percent targeted local governments. Moreover, some of the protests targeting the central government did not necessarily occur in Beijing. For example, some parents who lost their only child blamed the central government for the one-child policy, but they directed their action against local authorities. This reinforces the point that, as local governments are mostly responsible for dealing with social protests in China, their response dictates the opportunities for and outcomes of such protests. Governments at the city and county levels were targeted in 38 percent of the cases, whereas grassroots authorities at the township and village levels were targeted in another 14 percent. City and county governments were frequently targeted even though grievances were mostly caused by other local actors, including businesses.

Trends in Protests

Our data reveal a long and steady rise in mass actions until 2014, followed by a receding tide in later years (Figure 3).[17] The many persistent sources of conflict, such as urbanization and marketization, caused the grievances of various social groups. These grievances translated into action when mobilization became possible. Thus, we surmise that a combination of increasing provocations, combined with a relatively permissive political environment, brought about this long rising trend. The permissive environment had to do with the central government's tolerance of local protests, and the tolerance prevented local authorities from applying coercion at will. The constraint from above created opportunities for collective action (see Figure 1).

As far as the decline from 2015 is concerned, the causes may also be multiple. One is that strengthened censorship reduced reports on such incidents after 2014. This is possible because the government's control over the media was tightened after Xi came to power. Yet, given the limitations of available sources, it is difficult to assess to what degree strengthened censorship has reduced reporting on social protests in China. Our collection includes large-scale protests (more than 1,000 participants). Large-scale protests were less likely to be censored, and they can more accurately represent the trend in social protests. As Figure 3 shows, the distribution of such large actions from 2000 to 2017 exhibits a similar pattern that can be taken as confirming the general trend. The year

---

[17] Zhang and Pan's research shows that the peak was in late 2013, which was not greatly different from our finding (Zhang and Pan 2019).

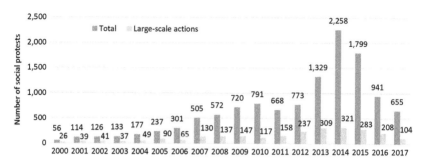

Figure 3 Social protests in China over time
Source: authors' collection

2014 saw the most large-scale protests (321) and the decline occurred from the next year (283).

A second possible reason for the decline is a decrease in sources of grievances that cause collective actions. Yet, it seems that sources of conflict remain widespread in China. For example, labor disputes have long been an important cause of social protests (Lee 2007; Chen 2020a), and these disputes remain large in number. According to the *Chinese Labor Statistical Yearbook* (2011–18), labor disputes accepted by mediation agencies increased from 600,865 in 2010 to 813,860 in 2015 (an increase of 35.4 percent), 828,410 in 2016, and 785,323 in 2017. There is a slight decline in the labor disputes from 2015 to 2017 (i.e., by 3.5 percent); however, Figure 3 indicates a drastic decrease (63.6 percent) in collective action over the same period. In other words, the decline in the sources of grievance may not be the major cause of the decline in collective action after 2015.

We do not have sufficient information to explain why collective action increased and reached a peak in the first two years of the Xi administration. One possible reason is what we might call an "imagined honeymoon" among the aggrieved in China. Lianjiang Li, Mingxing Liu, and Kevin O'Brien (2012) find that more petitioners went to Beijing in 2003 when former president Hu Jintao and former premier Wen Jiabao first came to power because these people believed that the new administration adopted a more populist leadership style. This belief was an "imagined honeymoon" because it could be false or unfounded. Indeed, coercion was soon adopted to stop petitioners from going to the national capital during the Hu–Wen administration. However, the people found that their belief was a false one only after many of them had taken action.

Some of the aggrieved people in China might have had the same belief in the Xi administration in its initial years. When he first came to power, Xi not only stressed anticorruption but also promised to provide the Chinese people with a better life (Yang 2012). In Xi's initial years, the aggrieved may have taken action with the expectation of receiving a sympathetic response from the new administration. However, a rise in collective action was not what the administration itself desired, as Xi was fully engaged in power consolidation right after he came to power. As a result, the administration in fact became less tolerant of social protests. As discussed in the next section, the decline in collective action was accompanied by the increased use of coercion during the Xi administration, which has issued policies discouraging defiant behavior and protest.

6 Applying Coercion

Chinese local governments do not have to repress all social protests, but coercion becomes an option when the perceived risks of repression are low or when the central government tolerates or encourages repression. Since 2014, the Chinese central authority has repeatedly signaled its emphasis on social control. In addition, Beijing has also coordinated repressive measures to deal with certain groups of people, such as rights-defense lawyers. Consequently, coercion has been more frequently used by local governments under the Xi administration than in earlier administrations. Against this background, incidents of collective action, especially large-scale ones, have begun to decline in the past few years.

The "Good-Emperor" Tactic and Its Implication for Resistance

In an authoritarian regime that consists of multiple levels of government, the central government can avoid being blamed for unpopular policies through decentralization (Weaver 1986). In China, by assigning blame-generating responsibilities to local governments or by scapegoating cadres at lower levels, the central government can protect its image as a "good emperor." When local officials cause popular grievances, the central government can protect its own image by denouncing and disciplining the former or by paying lip service to the demands of the aggrieved even if it lacks the resources or determination to solve the problems. Local officials who have caused citizen grievances then become the "bad guys" (O'Brien and Li 2007, 42–47). The central government's image-protecting measures can embolden citizens and encourage their resistance to local officials.

This "good-emperor" tactic was used by the Jiang Zemin and Hu–Wen administrations when they dealt with disputes between citizens and local governments. For example, when peasants faced severe financial burdens in the 1990s, the central government did not allocate financial resources to local governments to alleviate the fiscal shortages that were the fundamental cause of the burdens. Rather, it regulated local cadres' behavior and disciplined those responsible for egregious abuses. The central government then issued a policy in 1996 to limit peasants' tax burden to 5 percent of their income in the previous year.

An Chen (2008, 334–335) contends that central decrees concerning peasants' financial burdens amounted to little more than empty words or just a propaganda tactic aiming to appease discontented peasants. However, this symbolic gesture proved highly consequential because it legitimized peasant grievances and generated widespread "policy-based resistance" or "rightful resistance" (O'Brien and Li 2007). When local officials' tax collection caused peasant deaths, responsible cadres would be punished (Cai 2010, 174).

When local officials were disciplined, the punishment sent a clear message to peasants that the center always stood with them and was "angry" that "a few" rural officials had not implemented the center's policies protecting peasant interests (Chen, An 2008). Thus, when the central government was less tolerant toward local officials' abuse of power, it created opportunities for peasant resistance, though the resistance was not necessarily successful.

After Hu Jintao and Wen Jiabao came to power in 2002, they abolished the agricultural tax in 2004. However, their administration also discouraged collective petitions and decreed in 2005 that the number of participants in collective petitions should not exceed five. Yet, the central government did not prohibit people from presenting petitions to national authorities by skipping over local authorities. On January 4, 2011, Premier Wen Jiabao went to the National Complaints Bureau and talked to petitioners about their issues (Lu and Qing 2011). Although Wen's move might be dismissed as a political show, his gesture at least suggested that the central government was sticking to the mass line – keeping in close touch with the people and caring about their welfare. In contrast, the Xi administration does not seem to be using the "good-emperor" tactic. Instead, it has made explicit policies discouraging or repressing resistance.

Signaled Preferences of the Xi Administration

Ivan Franceschini and Elisa Nesossi (2018) find that in Xi's China, the authorities are using the law to exercise everyday control, closing the "policy windows" opened by Hu Jintao's leadership. Compared with earlier administrations under Jiang and Hu, Xi's administration is more tolerant of, or even encourages, local repression. The rise of the repressive regime in today's China may be tied to Xi's consolidation of political power. Xi purged a number of political rivals and perceived challengers after he came to power. The targets of the purge included a number of high-ranking officials, including Bo Xilai (former Party secretary of Chongqing), Zhou Yongkang (former Secretary of the Central Commission of Political and Legal Affairs and a member of the Politburo Standing Committee), and some military leaders. In addition, about 1.54 million cadres or party members were disciplined for corruption between 2012 and 2017.[18]

Xi's power consolidation efforts created a repressive political environment that has affected the behavior of local authorities. As these efforts require a stable political environment, a series of measures have been taken to ensure social stability. As mentioned earlier, grid management has become an important means of monitoring in China (Tang 2020). The Chinese government began to try the system and then promoted it in 2013. That year, the central authority promulgated a directive entitled "The Central Party Committee's Important Decisions on Comprehensive and Deepened Reform." This directive, for the first time, put forward grid management as an important means of "social governance."[19] Grid management aims to penetrate into and thereby monitor grassroots society, resolve conflict through multiple channels, and address conflict in the place of its occurrence. This system is expected to reduce popular contention and petitions.

Meanwhile, the social environment has become repressed. Journalists are pressured to resign themselves to being tools of the propaganda machinery, and influential social media accounts are either strictly censored or completely shut down (Buckley 2018). Schoolteachers are prohibited from discussing issues in class that are deemed politically sensitive. Party authorities have recruited college students as informants to monitor their instructors in class. Some university professors were reported by students and accused of having criticized the Party's rule. These instructors were given different types of discipline, ranging from being deprived of teaching opportunities to being warned or fired (*Washington Post* Editorial Board 2018).

Legal professionals who try to defend citizens pursuing their legitimate interests also have become targets of repression. Rights-defense lawyers in China offer critical support to citizens who have disputes with state agencies (Fu and Cullen 2008). However, the government may be aggrieved when lawyers provide defense in legal disputes with state agencies, leading to the lawyers being penalized. In July 2015, the Chinese government coordinated

---

[18] See the website of the Central Discipline Inspection Commission, www.ccdi.gov.cn/xxgk/hyzl/.

[19] "The Central Party Committee's Important Decisions on Comprehensive and Deepened Reform" (中共中央关于全面深化改革若干重大问题的决定), see the website of the Chinese government, www.gov.cn/jrzg/2013-11/15/content_2528179.htm. Grid management is also based on the so-called Fengqiao experience (枫桥经验), which means localizing conflict resolution.

a move targeting rights-defense lawyers, arresting around 300 rights lawyers, legal assistants, and activists from across the country (Gan 2015). An important cause of the arrests was the government's belief in the challenge posed by these lawyers. Penalizing lawyers in cases of administrative litigation is not rare in China (Liu and Halliday 2016), but it is uncommon for the national government to coordinate such a large-scale repressive move targeting lawyers.

Discouraging Resistance

The central government also made policies to discourage popular resistance, including collective action. A policy that is directly related to people's collective action is the central government's regulations on petitions. Petitions are an important mode of political participation in China, and collective petitions are the basic mode of collective action or social protests. When a group of people collectively approaches state authorities to present grievances, collective petitions sometimes escalate to more dramatic forms of collective action like large gatherings, demonstrations, blocking traffic, or even assaults on state agencies (Cai 2010; Chen 2012). For this reason, as mentioned earlier, the state council dictates that the number of participants in a collective petition should not exceed five.

During the Xi administration, presenting petitions to upper-level authorities has been explicitly discouraged. In 2014, the National Public Complaints and Proposals Administration (NPCPA; formerly called the National Complaints Bureau) promulgated a regulation prohibiting skip-level petitions (i.e., those circumventing local governments) and increased the difficulties faced by petitioners.[20] An NPCPA official admitted in 2014 that, among the petitions received by this bureau, approximately 90 percent belonged to the category of skip-level petitions. As petitions in Beijing exert pressure on the central government, officials dislike them. The 2014 directive indicated that the central authorities would no longer be accommodating petitioners. Consequently, whereas nearly 90 percent of the petitions to the NPCPA were accepted by the Bureau before May 2014, only 10 percent were accepted after the new regulation (Cheng 2015).

Moreover, petitioners seen as troublemakers were disciplined. Some petitioners have been accused of disrupting social order and were jailed for presenting petitions in the "wrong places." For example, a petitioner from a county

---

[20] Skip-level petitions (越级上访) refer to a petition mode in which the aggrieved go directly to the high-level authority like the national authority to present their grievances by bypassing local authorities.

in Fujian Province was convicted for causing disruption in places that are regarded as politically sensitive. Due to a dispute regarding forced home relocation, this person traveled to Beijing between May 2014 and January 2015 to file his petition. He presented his petition thirteen times near Zhongnanhai, where central leaders work, and thrice in front of the United Nations Development Program (Yan, Fameng 2018). In 2018, another petitioner from Shaanxi Province was sentenced to four and a half years in jail because her petitioning in Beijing between 2005 and 2017 had "caused disruptions" (Li 2018). When these cases were covered by the media, they signaled the government's discouragement of such petitions.

The Chinese government further regulated the behavior of petitioners in March 2019. That year, the Ministry of Public Security specified in great detail thirty-two situations in which petitioners could be disciplined. Under the rules, petitioners can be punished if they pursue unacceptable modes of petitioning, petitioning in prohibited places, or behaving in an unacceptable way when petitioning. Specifically, skip-level petitions are not allowed, trouble-making is not tolerated, and submitting materials collected in inappropriate or illegal ways is prohibited. Needless to say, organizing collective actions is not tolerated. To sum up, these regulations aim to ensure that Chinese citizens must present petitions in a peaceful and nonthreatening manner to designated state agencies.[21]

These regulations and incidents of repression signal the risk of "inappropriate" resistance. Local authorities do not always strictly enforce these rules, but the rules become the basis for repressing disobedient petitioners when necessary. For example, in April 2021, an 81-year-old man in Tongxu County in Henan Province was jailed; he had previously been sentenced to three years in jail in 2019 with a reprieve.[22] He was accused of causing disturbances when he made petitions because of a dispute over compensation for his land being taken away. He was later jailed after he gave interviews to journalists.

Local Response to Protests

When the central government signaled its preference for social control, local governments behaved accordingly. Given the central government's attitude toward citizens' rights defense, it may not be surprising that coercion has

---

[21] "The Ministry of Public Security Specifies the 32 Situations in which Petitioning Is Illegal" (公安部明确:这32种上访行为违法), https://k.sina.com.cn/article_1789250890_6aa5c d4a02000ecan.html.

[22] "An 81-Year-Old Man with a Suspended Prison Sentence Was Taken Away from His Ward and Jailed after Being Interviewed by a Journalist" (81岁老人上访被判缓刑, 因接受记者采访被 转实刑, 病房里被带走), www.163.com/dy/article/GLVVS9L80551OS2Q.html.

been used more frequently by local governments under the Xi administration. Coercion sometimes involves the deployment of police or armed police. In one case in January 2019, a large-scale protest occurred in Jinhu County in Jiangsu Province after official reports confirming at least 145 children in the county, aged between three months and four years old, had received expired polio vaccines. Local residents were angered because they believed that this practice could have been going on for years, and victims might far outnumber the 145. The county Party secretary who came out to talk to the protestors was surrounded and assaulted. In this situation, higher authorities mobilized armed police from neighboring counties, cities, and Shanghai to restore order in the county.[23]

Our data contain information on whether the police who dealt with protests arrested any participants. If arresting protest participants can be used as a proxy for repression, our data show a clear pattern that the Chinese government became increasingly repressive after 2012. As Table 3 shows, the police made arrests in 23.9 percent of the protests from 2000 to 2002, and in 27.4 percent of the protests from 2003 to 2012. In contrast, the police made arrests in 39 percent of protests from 2013 to 2017. Cases involving arrests increased from nearly 21.5 percent in 2013 to approximately 55.1 percent in 2015 and 49.4 percent in 2016. This large increase implies that the Xi administration tolerates local authorities' use of repression; intensified repression reflects the preference of the central authority, which is in line with the tightened social control discussed earlier.

The use of coercion by local governments is also reflected in the number of people who were charged with the crime of "obstructing the social management order."[24] This crime refers to activities that prevent state agencies, legal

Table 3 Repression during different administrations

Period	Cases (A)	Repressed cases (B)	B/A (%)
2000–2	289	69	23.9
2003–7	1,338	366	27.4
2008–12	3,488	956	27.4
2013–17	6,715	2,616	39.0
Total	11,830	4,007	33.9

Source: authors' collection

---

[23] Authors' interviews; Zhang 2019.
[24] The Chinese term for this crime is "妨害社会管理秩序罪."

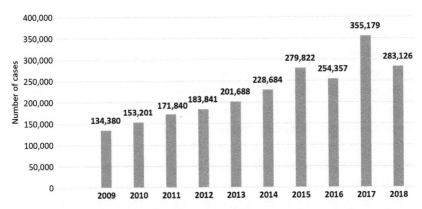

Figure 4 Cases of the crime of obstructing the social management order
Source: Compiled from the annual report of the Supreme Court.[25]

departments, and other organizations from conducting management activities. Not all of these activities concern social protests, but they include "instigating disturbances." As Figure 4 shows, the number of such cases tried in courts more than doubled from 134,380 in 2009 to 279,822 in 2015. Although there were also fluctuations in the number of cases between 2015 and 2018, the annual totals during this period are higher than in any year before 2014. It is unclear whether the increase was caused by more law violations or by stricter enforcement of the law, but charging a large number of people with this offense may have a deterrent effect.

Given the central government's encouragement of the use of coercion, local repression has begun to target social groups whose protests used to be tolerated. Such groups include college students and veterans, even when they do not raise political demands. One case that occurred in 2018 indicates the central and local governments' repressive attitude toward defiant behavior by college students (Kuo 2018). Beginning in May 2018, workers at Jasic Technologies, a factory in Shenzhen, attempted to follow the legal process to form a union, but their efforts were met with government repression. In July of the same year, the company and the district union denounced the workers' efforts as illegal; the company had hastily established a sham union to forestall the workers' efforts. Resisting workers were either reassigned or fired.

After the case drew public attention, the workers received support from college students from universities in Guangdong and other places, including Beijing. When workers and supporters protested, they faced coordinated repression.

---

[25] See the website of the Chinese Supreme Court, http://gongbao.court.gov.cn/ArticleList.html? serial_no=sftj.

These young activists learned of the workers' plight from internet messaging apps and took up their cause, with hundreds speaking out online in support, and about forty students and recent graduates traveling to Guangdong despite warnings from universities. Local authorities became hostile toward these young people. On August 24, riot police broke into an apartment where members of the support group were staying and arrested about fifty people. The same day, several supporters in Beijing were also arrested.

The repression of students continued. Chinese police in at least five cities arrested recent graduates of elite universities, including Beijing University, in early November 2018. At least a dozen young activists who participated in the national campaign for workers' rights went missing. The government's repression appeared to be an effort to silence one of the most active and highly visible student protests in years. On the night of November 9, several men who claimed to be police officers went to Beijing University to arrest Zhang Shengye, a recent graduate who had actively participated in the campaign. Zhang had been coordinating efforts to find activists who had been detained in unknown places by the authorities (Hernández 2018).

Protests by veterans have also been repressed. Over the years, Chinese veterans have staged a series of demonstrations in cities, including Beijing (Diamant 2009; O'Brien and Diamant 2015). In our collection of 11,830 cases of collective action from 2000 to 2017, veterans staged 278 protests from 2005 to 2017, of which seventy-seven were large-scale protests. In 2016, thousands of veterans staged a quiet sit-in outside the headquarters of the Central Military Commission, which was reportedly the largest protest initiated by veterans in China since 1949. These veterans' protests recurred in 2017 and persisted after the Ministry of Veterans Affairs was created in 2018. Some of the 57 million veterans had raised various types of welfare demands, such as job allocations and compensation.

Yet, the Chinese government seems to have become less tolerant of veterans' protests, partly because veterans have organized cross-region collective actions. In June 2018, thousands of veterans joined a five-day protest in Zhenjiang City in Jiangsu Province when rumors spread that at least one veteran had been beaten while seeking government help. The protest ended when the Jiangsu government sent in hundreds of armed police to disperse the group, resulting in several veterans being injured and hospitalized. Veterans claimed that "assaults on veterans are a public humiliation for China's military" (Chan 2018). Reportedly, after May 2018, multiple assaults were staged against veterans by "gangsters and thugs" hired by local officials to "maintain stability" in the provinces of Guangdong, Sichuan, Hunan, Hainan, Henan, Anhui, and Liaoning, among other places.

In December 2018, local authorities in Shandong Province arrested ten people who were accused of organizing a "serious attack" on police officers during a veterans' protest in Pingdu City in October 2018. The authorities claimed that, during the assembly of hundreds of veterans led by ten people, the participants acted violently toward the police and smashed police vehicles. It was claimed that thirty-four people, including an unknown number of police officers, had been wounded in the violence, and that a police bus and three private cars were destroyed. These ten people were then arrested and charged with crimes including obstructing the enforcement of the law, intentional harm, mobilizing the masses to disrupt public order, and provoking disturbances. The arrest and trial of these ten activists were widely reported in major national media outlets, including China Central Television, the *People's Daily*, and the *People's Liberation Army Daily*, apparently as a warning against veterans who intended to stage similar collective actions in the future. Another nine participants in the protest in Zhenjiang were also arrested and sent to trial (Yan, Alice 2018).

Although repression was also used in the Jiang Zemin and Hu Jintao administrations, coercion coordinated by the central government seems to be more common under Xi. As discussed earlier, the arrests of rights-defense lawyers in 2015, the repression of labor protests in Shenzhen in 2018, and the repression of veterans in recent years all involved the coordination of central authorities.

Effect of Coercion

While coercion has been more frequently used under the Xi administration (Table 3), incidents of collective action have also begun to decline. We do not have sufficient evidence to conclude that the decline was caused solely by repression; however, as discussed earlier, the signaled preference of the central government and its coordinated moves created a repressive environment that was not conducive to the mobilization of collective action, especially large-scale ones. The decline in collective action likely resulted from a combination of measures (see Section 3), including strengthened state monitoring, early intervention, and sanctioning. For example, the grid-management system began to be widely adopted from 2014, and many actions of resistance were nipped in the bud before they escalated into street protests.[26]

The collective action of petitioners serves as an example. As discussed earlier, the central government began to discourage petitions after 2014. According to our data (Table 4), collective actions staged by petitioners

---

[26] Conversation with a Chinese researcher who conducted dispute resolution in China, August 23, 2021.

declined dramatically from 2015. Petitioners' collective actions totaled 84 in 2012, then 226 in 2013, and 263 in 2014, but these actions declined to 134 in 2015 (falling by 49 percent), and further to 80 in 2016 and to 12 in 2019. There could be other reasons for the decrease in petitioners' collective actions, such as the strict censorship of reports on such collective actions. However, the central government's attitude toward petitioners was indicative of its tolerance of local repression.

Reinforcing the findings from our own data, the China Labor Bulletin also reports a sharp decline in large-scale collective actions. As presented in Table 4, similar to the pattern shown in our data (Figure 3), large-scale actions included in this data set rose from 25 in 2011 to 98 in 2014, and then began to decline from 2015. From 2017 to 2020, the number was consistently below 13. If the assumption that large-scale protests are more difficult to cover up is plausible, strict censorship may not be the primary reason for the decline in large-scale protests. A more plausible cause is the risks and difficulties involved in mobilizing large-scale action. Leaders of large-scale actions can be accused of organizing people to disrupt public order.

For example, in one case that we collected, a worker was arrested and then put in jail for twenty-one months in 2016 under the charge of amassing the people to disrupt social order. The real reason was that he led workers in a factory in Guangzhou to hold several strikes between 2014 and 2015. The

Table 4 Collective action in urban China (2011–20)

Year	Total actions	Large-scale actions (≥1,000 people)	Petitioners' collective actions
2011	203	25	46
2012	384	50	84
2013	647	62	226
2014	1,358	98	263
2015	2,775	83	134
2016	2,670	41	80
2017	1,258	1	94
2018	1,706	13	66
2019	1,385	3	12
2020	800	11	No data
2021	1,029	11	No data

Sources: "Total actions" and "large-scale actions" were retrieved from the website of the China Labor Bulletin, https://maps.clb.org.hk. Petitioners' collective actions were collected by the authors.

last strike was joined by more than 1,000 workers in the factory. Some protest leaders were also punished even though the actions that they led were smaller in scale. In another case, four peasants led a protest involving more than a hundred villagers stemming from a land dispute in their village in Anhui Province in 2019. These peasants attempted to stop construction on land taken away from their village because of a dispute over compensation. In the end, two peasants were detained, and the other two were released on parole.

The central and local governments believe that coercion is an effective measure of silencing the aggrieved. One example is the government's handling of the investors of P2P (peer-to-peer lending) platforms in China from the late 2010s to the early 2020s. During this period, a large number of P2P platforms went bankrupt and many who invested in them lost most or all of their principal. In one case, the Ai Qian Jin platform, the number of victims reached 370,000, with total losses of 23 billion yuan. When these people attempted to stage resistance, they were threatened and repressed by the police. Some people who attempted to go to Beijing to petition were detained on their way, a common tactic of local governments (Mai 2019).

Despite the large numbers of investors who had lost their savings, they were unable to stage a forceful collective action. With censorship, the sufferings of these investors no longer attracted the attention of the public. And, after all, this group of victims was still a minority in a population of 1.4 billion. Thus, the government could ignore them and use repression without causing widespread resentment. Coercion is likely to be used to deal with aggrieved investors in the future simply because the cost to the government of compensating them would be too high. As the central government is also aware of local governments' financial difficulties, the latter do not face big risks when they threaten, arrest, or imprison resisters.

Coercion has not prevented all collective actions, especially small-scale ones, in China. Small-scale actions are more difficult to prevent because mobilizing such action can be discreet. However, small-scale actions are less disruptive, and they are mostly reactive or defensive, focusing on low-politics issues. Yet, when coercion becomes persistent, both the scale and frequency of collective action decline.

7 Understanding Contention and Stability in China

This Element has shown that social protests have recurred in China over the past two decades, and collective action is an important mode of political participation for various social groups. However, these many incidents have not threatened the political stability of the country. Two conditions must be met for social protests to cause regime collapse. One is the rise of focal issues, such as a worsened economy, that cause widespread grievances in society and are then accompanied by triggering events (Castells 2015). The other is hesitancy among coercive forces like the police or the military. The Chinese government has managed to ensure social stability by containing grievances, shoring up public support for the regime, applying coercion to deter and contain collective action, and preventing a serious split among the political elite.

In China, partly because of decentralization, grievances tend to be specific to certain localities and social groups. Some common grievances vary in their degree of severity across the country. By preventing the accumulation and spread of grievances, the government limits the size of the aggrieved population and avoids any particular issue becoming a focus. However, accommodating the aggrieved requires resources, which are not always available, especially in economic downturns. Coercion remains the crucial means available to the government when it lacks the resources for accommodation. Social and political stability in China has been achieved through both legitimacy building and coercion.

Grievances and Social Stability

Regime-challenging collective actions are often triggered by focal issues that can be political or socioeconomic. Such issues unite people because they reflect their shared concerns or interests. More often than not, focal grievances concern people's daily lives. For example, economic grievances like unemployment and high inflation, together with popular resentment against the government for other issues, such as corruption, were important causes of the Jasmine Revolution in Tunisia and the uprising in Egypt (Castells 2015). Thus, authoritarian governments are strongly motivated to reduce grievances in society even if they are not able to achieve this.

In China, government policies and practices have caused the grievances of various social groups, but these grievances have failed to become focal issues for two reasons. One is that grievances are generally localized. Citizens' grievances can be community or locality specific. A direct outcome of this local variation is that citizens may delink their grievances from the political system and attribute them to local authorities. The other is that those who are economically disadvantaged may attribute their plight to their lack of marketable skills instead of the government (Blecher 2002). For example, Whyte (2010) argues that most Chinese people accept the present inequalities as individually earned, rather than the result of an unfair economic structure. Thus, social justice is not a major issue. Delinking grievances from the political system protects regime legitimacy.

Certain grievances can be common across the country, but they vary in severity or are group-specific. For example, when peasants protested against financial burdens from the 1990s to the early 2000s, peasants in the middle part of China suffered the most and protested more often than those in the eastern part of the country (Bernstein and Lü 2003). When the Chinese government carried out the industrial restructuring from the late 1990s to the early 2000s, tens of millions of workers were laid off. But local governments faced varied degrees of pressure when dealing with the layoffs. Local authorities in the three northeastern provinces – Liaoning, Jilin, and Heilongjiang – faced the most pressure, not only because they had more laid-off workers but also because they had limited resources. These local governments faced more pressure arising from worker protests than many others (Lee 2007; Hurst 2009; Cai 2010).

The government has tried to prevent the accumulation of grievances by addressing some of the sources of trouble. When certain issues cause widespread and persistent grievances across the country, they are often tied to the central government's policies or practices. In these circumstances, the national government becomes responsive but in different ways for the sake of protecting its legitimacy and ensuring social stability (Heurlin 2017). The central authorities may strengthen the enforcement of policies favoring local residents, or abolish unpopular policies. For example, housing demolition caused numerous disputes and incidents of resistance in China because of the low compensation paid to homeowners. Citizen resistance and high-profile suicides among homeowners in Nanjing and Beijing in 2003 prompted the Chinese central government to adjust its policies with respect to the compensation given to homeowners (Cai 2010).

The central and provincial governments may also offer help to resource-deficient local governments to reduce grievances and ensure social stability. For example, the government of Siping City in Jilin Province had limited financial resources to address the many grievances in the city. As presented in Table 5, its fiscal revenues in 2015 and 2016 fell far below its expenditures. As a result, the city government had to rely on subsidies from the central and provincial authorities to deal with local petitioners. Siping received financial assistance from both the central and provincial governments in 2015, and aid from the provincial government in 2016. The city government used its stability-preservation budget to solve sixty-four petition cases and used financial assistance from the provincial government to close another forty-one cases in 2016 (The Editorial Committee of Siping Gazette 2016, 91).

Variation in the severity of grievances inhibits cross-region collective action, but does not preclude it altogether. There is always a possibility that focal issues may arise. Authoritarian governments can survive political crises arising from

Table 5 Budgeting for conflict resolution, Siping City, Jilin Province

	2015	2016
Petition-resolution fund (million yuan)	15.16	13.5
Provided by the central government	3.0	–
Provided by the provincial government	9.16	10.5
City's stability-maintaining budget	3.0	3.0
City finance (million yuan)		
Fiscal revenue	600.23	600.34
Fiscal expenditures	2,200.11	2,600.13
Shortfall	1,500.88	1,900.79

Sources: Siping Yearbook 2016, p. 36; Siping Yearbook 2017, p. 91; Siping Statistical Yearbook 2017, pp. 176–177

social protests if they retain strong power and/or a high level of legitimacy or worthiness of respect (see Section 4). As the Chinese party-state still enjoys legitimacy and support, it is motivated to use a combination of legitimacy building and coercion to ensure its exclusive political rule.

Public Support and Regime Stability

The lack of focal (economic) issues in China can also be attributed to the fast economic growth in the past few decades, which has created a large number of beneficiaries. In other words, economic achievements and propaganda have allowed the government to shore up strong support for its rule, support that is shared across many social strata (Chen 2004; Tang 2005; Wright 2010; Dickson 2016). Economic success enables the party-state to form an implicit exchange relationship between the regime and the people. The regime provides economic benefits and social order to the people in exchange for their acceptance of the regime (Cook 1993).

Moreover, many of the beneficiaries work in the public sector directly under the party-state. For example, a survey of 3,017 residents in Beijing, Shanghai, and Guangzhou between 2014 and 2015 shows that 1,497 (or 49.6 percent) belong to the "middle-level stratum" (Liang and Zhang 2016). Among this group, those whose employment is connected to the party-state account for about 44 percent. These people work in Party and government agencies, state-owned enterprises, collective firms, and government-funded agencies. In other words, a significant number of people in China depend on the party-state for their comfortable incomes and secure benefits. People working in private businesses and foreign companies account for about 47 percent; these people too are economic beneficiaries of the regime, albeit less directly.

A similar exchange relationship also exists between the party-state and academia. As Elizabeth Perry (2020, 1) writes:

> As in the imperial past, authoritarian rule in China today is buttressed by a pattern of educated acquiescence, with academia acceding to political compliance in exchange for the many benefits conferred upon it by the state. The role of educated acquiescence in enabling Chinese authoritarianism highlights the contributions of a cooperative academy to authoritarian durability.

These economic beneficiaries tend to accept or echo the Party's propaganda or discourse hegemony about the comparative advantages of authoritarian rule. Thus, the new middle class is unlikely to serve as an agent or supporter of fundamental political change toward democracy "in major part due to their close and dependent relationship with the current party-state as well as their satisfaction with their own social and economic conditions under the current regime" (Chen and Lu 2011, 705). These people are not eager to see regime change or democratization in China (Chen 2002). People widely believe that stability benefits them. In a 1999 survey of 1,820 people, 59 percent agreed with the statement that "The most important condition for our country's progress is political stability. Democratization under the current conditions would only lead to chaos" (Tang 2005, 71).

It is not rare that people in authoritarian regimes uphold social order. Seweryn Bialer writes that in the former Soviet Union, the fear of disorder and the attachment to societal order were valued not only by political leaders and elites but also by the people:

> Undeniably, the Russian people in all walks of life fear the chaos and disorder they sense directly below the surface of their lives; they fear the potential of elemental explosions of violence and rage that mark their historical past and occupy a central place in their history textbooks; they prize and yearn for strong government, the *khoziain* or boss who will ward off the *smuta*, the "time of troubles." (Bialer 1986, 146)

In China, the public's fear of chaos arising from regime transition helps the party-state maintain its discourse hegemony concerning the irreplaceable role of the CCP. This hegemony is also strengthened because of propaganda and nationalism that is time and again mobilized by the government. As Ki Deuk Hyun and Jinhee Kim find, online political expression functions to maintain the status quo in the sense that it enhances people's general support for the Chinese system. "Just as the CCP intends, nationalism enhanced by online political expression operates as the main device to reinforce public acceptance and vindication of current social configurations in China" (Hyun and Kim 2015, 14).

Some people accept authoritarian rule as an exchange for benefits, whereas others truly believe in the legitimacy of the Party's rule. In recent years, these supporters commonly square off against regime critics in polarized discussions over issues that involve the government. Regime supporters come from all social groups, including public servants, school or university teachers, and those working in the private sector. Regime critics, including loyal critics who still accept authoritarian rule, are frequently accused of being pro-America or of ignoring the great achievements of the party-state. Critics accuse supporters of upholding the "illusory collective" while showing no mercy to the poor and the unfortunate.[27] The distribution or proportion of these two groups of people in society remains unknown; regime supporters far outnumber regime critics in social media like WeChat and Weibo, though this no doubt reflects censorship.

For example, in the case of the coronavirus that was initially identified in Wuhan in China in 2019 and then spread throughout the world thereafter, heated debates about the Chinese government's responsibility appeared online. Regime supporters accepted and disseminated the conspiracy theory that the virus originated in the United States and was introduced to China by members of the US Army who visited Wuhan for sports games (Meyers 2020). Regime critics rejected this conspiracy theory and argued that it was the Chinese government's attempt to avoid responsibility for mishandling the epidemic at the initial stage. Because of censorship, messages criticizing the government or disclosing so-called negative information were generally prohibited (Erickson 2018). Those who posted such messages were warned or detained. The discourse of the government and regime supporters enjoys decisive advantages, creating a propaganda hegemony among the population. Discourse hegemony lends support to the party-state's rule, discourages regime critics, and contributes to regime legitimacy and stability.

Coercion and Stability

Although the Chinese central government still enjoys high political trust among the citizenry, there are always aggrieved people whose interests have suffered harm in some way. As well, there are always regime critics who do not accept authoritarian rule. As the government is unable to accommodate all forms of discontent, repression remains the crucial and ultimate means of silencing the aggrieved. Repression deters and contains collective action over economic

---

[27] "They show incomparable love for the illusory collective, but are indifferent and cruel to specific individuals" (对虚幻的集体无比热爱, 对具体个人冷漠残忍; 对宏大叙事不亦乐乎, 对个体悲剧视若无睹。). This criticism of regime supporters was raised by a number of regime critics, including Fang Fang, a well-known writer in Wuhan who published her diaries during the coronavirus epidemic. For her diary, see https://chinadigitaltimes.net/space.

issues while even more aggressively silencing overtly political actions. Repression becomes the option when the government lacks the resources to meet the demands of the aggrieved or when the central authorities perceive a threat of social unrest. Consistent repression creates a harsh environment in which protestors face grave risks if they mobilize collective action against the will of the government.

In China, repressing protestors with legitimate claims weakens the government's image and contradicts its official claim of serving the people. The central government is in a good position to protect itself because it generally makes repressive policies rather than carry out repression, except for political cases like the Falun Gong. It is mostly local governments that directly enforce coercive measures. In other words, the central government can shift the blame-generating responsibility to local agents.

However, people may still come to realize that the repressive climate is the policy choice of the central government. The central and local governments can reduce the damage repression causes to their legitimacy by "outsourcing repression" to local thugs (Ong 2018) or by politicizing citizens' action. Chinese protestors generally do not raise political demands, but their action can still be politicized and criminalized by the government. Some protestors have been accused of staging regime-challenging action or of subverting the government. Politicizing citizens' behaviors serves the interests of the government in two ways. First, politicizing contentious behavior justifies the use of repression and minimizes the risks that repression carries for local governments (Cai 2010, 130). Second, by politicizing popular resistance, the government can avoid being blamed for its failure in governance. It shifts the blame to protestors who are accused of challenging the regime or working with overseas forces to overthrow the communist regime.

Blaming protestors is possible because the government controls the media and discourse. The government's control over the media also allows it to censor information about social protests that have occurred, though timely censorship is not always possible because of the wide use of social media. As protestors are a small segment of the population, information control can suffice to protect the government's image when repression is applied. In other cases, if local governments use excessive repression, the central government can avert popular anger by disciplining individual local officials. Thus, the political hierarchy allows the central government to use repression while limiting the damage to its image.

8 Conclusion

China has been undergoing important socioeconomic changes over the past two decades, such as urbanization, industrial restructuring, and marketization.

These changes have caused numerous social conflicts, and social protests have therefore kept occurring. Collective action in China is an indication of the weak power of the citizens because they often lack institutionalized channels to protect their interests from being ignored or violated in the first place. Social protests then become a mode of political participation on the part of these citizens who seek to influence "the results of governmental policy" rather than policymaking or the selection of government officials (Shi 1997, 22). Chinese citizens sometimes do succeed in protecting their interests though collective action.

Tasked with the responsibility of handling social conflict by taking collective action, Chinese local governments have taken multiple measures for this purpose. Their responses to social protests include concessions, turning a blind eye, temporizing, and repression. Each of these responses can help silence the aggrieved, but each has limitations. Chinese local governments do not always rely on repression to silence protestors, but coercion remains a crucial method because it limits the frequency and scale of collective action.

This Element demonstrates how the Chinese central government contains social protests by shaping the political opportunity structure facing the aggrieved through coercion. In the Chinese political hierarchy, Chinese local officials are answerable to higher-level authorities, including the central government. The opportunity for collective action is therefore shaped by the stance taken by the central authorities. When the central government tolerates social protests, local governments face constraints if they want to use repression. In these circumstances, opportunities for collective action exist. If the central government is reluctant to see social protests, local governments face low risks when applying repression. Consequently, opportunities for collective action diminish.

Concern for regime legitimacy and the need to collect information are believed to be important reasons for the central authority to sometimes tolerate local protests (O'Brien and Li 2007; Cai 2010; Lorentzen 2013). These constraints imply that the central government does not always encourage the use of repression, and it may issue accommodating policies to address citizen grievances. Accommodating the interests of the aggrieved prevents the accumulation and spread of grievances. Over the years, the Chinese government has revised or made policies to address certain sources of social conflict, such as peasants' financial burdens and undercompensated housing demolition.

The central government, however, faces few limits and only soft constraints in its approach toward protests, and sanctions or coercion remains the crucial method of ensuring social and political stability in China. This Element highlights that the central government's attitude toward protesting groups is not fixed. Instead, its preference changes over time because of the political and/or socioeconomic environment that shapes political leaders' priorities. When the central authority feels that the threat arising from social protests is severe, the loss of legitimacy due to repression is no longer a constraint. Coercion becomes the main option. When the central government signals its preference, local authorities behave accordingly.

In recent years, incidents of collective action in China have not disappeared, but their numbers have declined somewhat, particularly for large-scale actions. This decline is very likely associated with government coercion. Compared with earlier administrations, the Xi administration seems to be less tolerant of collective action; protestors have been arrested at higher rates under Xi. Coercion does not deter all collective action because threats can still trigger reactive resistance. However, coercion can reduce the frequency and scale of collective action. Large-scale collective actions have been rare in recent years because such actions often require mobilization and thereby carry risks for the organizers.

In China in the past few decades, the sources of conflict have kept changing, and grievances have become specific to certain localities or social groups. The government's multiple measures ensure social stability amid these grievances. On one hand, concessions and policy adjustments prevent the accumulation of grievances or remove the sources of conflict. At any particular time, the number of aggrieved people is limited when compared with the large population of the country, much of which still has a high level of trust in the regime. As many people have benefited from the economic growth over the past few decades, they become regime supporters if their interests have not been violated. Or, even if they have, these people may not blame the central government or the regime.

On the other hand, coercion undermines the mobilization capacity of the aggrieved while increasing the risks that they face in attempting collective action. In an atomized society, there is a lack of solidarity among the citizens because of state control and the lack of formal mobilization networks such as religious or social associations. When both the Chinese central and local governments become hostile toward collective action, the political space for social protests is drastically reduced. This is particularly true for actions deemed political challenges, such as those taken by the Falun Gong sect.

A combination of accommodating practices and repressive tactics, together with a fragmented society, allow the Chinese government to achieve social stability without the repression sacrificing a great amount of regime legitimacy. However, this success so far by no means implies that the Chinese government is immune to pressure arising from popular grievances. Both the accommodating policies and the operation of the repressive apparatus require resources that can be obtained only through economic growth. However, economic growth is not always possible. Although economic downturns do not always cause regime collapse in authoritarian states (Geddes 1999), the rising numbers of the disaffected may put the elaborate institutions and practices of protest management discussed in these pages to a more difficult test.

References

Abrahamian, Ervand. 1982. *Iran between Two Revolutions*. Princeton, NJ: Princeton University Press.

Bai, Xi. 2009. *Kaiguo da tugai* (Land reform during the Founding of a New China). Beijing: The Party History Press.

Balkin, Jack. 2004. "Respect-Worthy: Frank Michelman and the Legitimate Constitution." *Tulsa Law Review* 39: 485–509.

Bellin, Eva. 2012. "Reconsidering the Robustness of Authoritarianism in the Middle East: Lessons from the Arab Spring." *Comparative Political Studies* 44 (2): 127–149.

Bernstein, Thomas, and Xiaobo Lü. 2003. *Taxation without Representation in Contemporary China*. New York: Cambridge University Press.

Bialer, Seweryn. 1986. *Stalin's Successors: Leadership, Stability and Change in the Soviet Union*. New York: Cambridge University Press.

Blecher, Marc. 2002. "Hegemony and Workers' Politics in China." *China Quarterly* 170: 283–303.

Bray, David. 2006. "Building 'Community': New Strategies of Governance in Urban China." *Economy and Society* 35 (4): 530–549.

Buckley, Chris. 2018. "China Gives Communist Party More Control Over Policy and Media." *New York Times*, March 21.

Cai, Yongshun. 2008a. "Power Structure and Regime Resilience: Contentious Politics in China." *British Journal of Political Science* 38 (3): 411–432.

2008b. "Local Governments and the Suppression of Popular Resistance in China." *China Quarterly* 193: 24–42.

2010. *Collective Resistance in China: Why Popular Protests Succeed or Fail*. Stanford, CA: Stanford University Press.

2019. "Information as a Source of Pressure: Local Government and Information Management in China." *Interdisciplinary Political Studies* 5 (2): 477–509.

Cai, Yongshun, and Titi Zhou. 2016. "New Information Communication Technologies and Social Protest in China." *Asian Survey* 56 (4): 731–753.

2019. "Online Political Participation in China: Local Government and Differentiated Response." *China Quarterly* 238: 331–352.

Calhoun, Craig. 2013. "Occupy Wall Street in Perspective." *British Journal of Sociology* 64 (1): 26–38.

Castells, Manuel. 2015. *Networks of Outrage and Hope: Social Movements in the Internet Age*. Cambridge: Polity Press.

Chan, Chris King-Chi, and Pun Ngai. 2009. "The Making of a New Working Class? A Study of Collective Actions of Migrant Workers in South China." *China Quarterly* 198: 287–303.

Chan, Minnie. 2018. "Chinese Military Veterans' Rally for Better Welfare Ends as Armed Police Move In." *South China Morning Post*, June 24.

Chen, An. 2002. "Capitalist Development, Entrepreneurial Class, and Democratization in China." *Political Science Quarterly* 117 (3): 401–422.

2008. "The 1994 Tax Reform and Its Impact on China's Rural Fiscal Structure." *Modern China* 34 (3): 303–343.

Chen, Baifeng. 2013. "Quntixing shefa naofang qiji fazhi" (Law-Related Collective Action and Legal Solutions). *Fazhi yu shehui fazhan* (Rule of Law and Social Development) 4: 17–28.

Chen, Chih-Jou Jay. 2009. "Growing Social Unrest and Emergent Protest Groups in China." In Hsin-Huang Michael Hsiao and Cheng-Yi Lin (eds.), *Rise of China: Beijing's Strategies and Implications for the Asia-Pacific*. London: Routledge, pp. 87–106.

2020a. "A Protest Society Evaluated: Popular Protests in China, 2000–2019." *Mobilization: An International Quarterly* 25 (SI): 641–660.

2020b. "Peasant Protests over Land Seizures in Rural China." *Journal of Peasant Studies* 47 (6): 1327–1347.

Chen, Chiu-Jou Jay, and Yongshun Cai. 2001. "Upward Targeting and Social Protests in China." *Journal of Contemporary China* 30 (130): 511–525.

Chen, Feng. 2008. "Worker Leaders and Framing Factory-Based Resistance." In Kevin O'Brien (ed.), *Popular Protest in China*. Cambridge, MA: Harvard University Press, pp. 88–107.

Chen, Feng, and Yi Kang. 2016. "Disorganized Popular Contention and Local Institutional Building in China: A Case Study in Guangdong." *Journal of Contemporary China* 25 (100): 596–612.

Chen, Jie. 2004. *Popular Political Support in Urban China*. Stanford, CA: Stanford University Press.

Chen, Jie, and Chunlong Lu. 2011. "Democratization and the Middle Class in China: The Middle Class's Attitudes toward Democracy." *Political Research Quarterly* 64 (3): 705–719.

Chen, Xi. 2012. *Social Protest and Contentious Authoritarianism in China*. New York: Cambridge University Press.

2013. "The Rising Cost of Stability." *Journal of Democracy* 24 (1): 57–64.

2017. "Origins of Informal Coercion in China." *Politics and Society* 45 (1): 67–89.

Chen, Ying, and Chih-Jou Jay Chen. 2021. "The State Owes Us: Social Exclusion and Collective Actions of China's Bereaved Parents." *Modern China* 47 (6): 740–764.

Cheng, Shuwen. 2015. "Guojia xinfangju: jueda duoshu jinjing shangfang bei ju shouli" (Most Petitions Presented to the Central Authority Were Rejected). *Nanfang dushi bao* (*South Metropolis News*), September 29.

Chow, Ching-wen. 1960. *Ten Years of Storm: The True Story of the Communist Regime in China*. New York: Holt, Rinehart and Winston.

Chung, Jae Ho. 2012. "Managing Political Crises in China." In Jae Ho Chung (ed.), *China's Crisis Management*. London: Routledge, pp. 25–42.

Cook, Linda. 1993. *The Soviet Social Contract and Why It Failed: Welfare Policy and Workers' Politics from Brezhnev to Yeltsin*. Cambridge, MA: Harvard University Press.

Deng, Luwen. 2014. "Ruhe zouchu 'zhengling buchu zhongnanhai' de kunjing" (How to Solve the Plight of 'Central Policies Are Ignored outside Zhongnanhai.'" *Chinese Business News Daily*, June 28.

Deng Xiaoping. 1993. *Deng Xiaoping Wenxuan* (A Collection of Deng Xiaoping's Works). Beijing: The People's Press.

Deng, Yanhua, and Kevin O'Brien. 2013. "Relational Repression in China: Using Social Ties to Demobilize Protesters." *China Quarterly* 215: 533–552.

2014. "Societies of Senior Citizens and Popular Protest in Rural Zhejiang." *China Journal* 71: 172–188.

Deng, Yanhua, and Guobin Yang. 2013. "Pollution and Protest in China: Environmental Mobilization in Context." *China Quarterly* 214: 321–336

Diamant, Neil. 2009. *Embattled Glory: Veterans, Military Families, and the Politics of Patriotism in China, 1949–2007*. Lanham, MD: Rowman and Littlefield.

Dickson, Bruce. 2016. *The Dictator's Dilemma: The Chinese Communist Party's Strategy for Survival*. New York: Oxford University Press.

Dziak, John. 1988. *Chekisty: A History of the KGB*. Lexington, MA: Lexington Books.

Earl, Jennifer, Andrew Martin, John McCarthy, and Sarah Soule. 2004. "The Use of Newspaper Data in the Study of Collective Action." *Annual Review of Sociology* 30: 65–80.

Edin, Maria. 2003. "State Capacity and Local Agent Control in China: CCP Cadre Management from a Township Perspective." *China Quarterly* 173: 35–52.

The Editorial Committee of Siping Gazette. 2016. *Siping Yearbook*. Changchun: Jilin Literature and History Press.

The Editorial Group of Red Flag Press. 2005. *Goujian shehuizhuyi hexie shehui dacankao* (Reference on the Building of a Socialist Harmonious Society). Beijing: Red Flag Press.

Ekiert, Grzegorz. 1996. *The State against Society: Political Crises and Their Aftermath in East Central Europe*. Princeton, NJ: Princeton University Press.

Elfstrom, Manfred. 2019. "Two Steps Forward, One Step Back: Chinese State Reactions to Labour Unrest." *The China Quarterly* 240: 855–879.

2021. *Workers and Change in China: Resistance, Repression, Responsiveness*. Cambridge: Cambridge University Press.

Erickson, Amanda. 2018. "'Here They Come Again': Chinese Police Arrest Dissident Professor during On-Air Interview." *Washington Post*, August 3.

Feng, Emily. 2018. "Security Spending Ramped up in China's Restive Xinjiang Region." *Financial Times*, March 13.

Franceschini, Ivan, and Elisa Nesossi. 2018. "State Repression of Chinese Labor NGOs: A Chilling Effect?" *China Journal* 80: 111–129.

French, Howard. 2005. "20 Reported Killed as Chinese Unrest Escalates." *New York Times*, December 9.

Fu, Diana. 2017. "Fragmented Control: Governing Contentious Labor Organizations in China." *Governance* 30: 445–462.

2018. *Mobilizing without the Masses: Control and Contention in China*. New York: Cambridge University Press.

Fu, Hualing, and Richard Cullen. 2008. "Weiquan (Rights Protection) Lawyering in an Authoritarian State: Building a Culture of Public-Interest Lawyering." *China Journal* 59: 111–127.

Gan, Nector. 2015. "Isolated, Tortured and Mentally Scarred . . . The Plight of China's Persecuted Human Rights Lawyers." *South China Morning Post*, July 13.

Geddes, Barbara. 1999. "What Do We Know about Democratization after Twenty Years?" *Annual Review of Political Science* 2: 115–144.

Geddes, Barbara, Joseph Wright, and Erica Frantz. 2018. *How Dictatorships Work: Power, Personalization, and Collapse*. New York: Cambridge University Press.

Göbel, Christian. 2021. "The Political Logic of Protest Repression in China." *Journal of Contemporary China* 30 (128): 169–185

Göbel, Christian, and Christoph Steinhardt. 2019. "Better Coverage, Less Bias: Using Social Media to Measure Protest in Authoritarian Regimes," Department of East Asian Studies, University of Vienna.

Goldstone, Jack, and Charles Tilly. 2001. "Threat (and Opportunity): Popular Action and State Response in the Dynamics of Contentious Action."

In Ronald Aminzade et al. (eds.), *Silence and Voice in the Study of Contentious Politics*. New York: Cambridge University Press, pp. 179–194.

Gong, Shengsheng, and Zhang Tao. 2013. "Zhongguo 'aizhengcun' shikong fenbu bianqian" (Research on the Change in the Distribution of Cancer Villages across Time and Space in China). *China Population, Resource and Environment* 9: 156–164.

Graham-Harrison. 2014. "I'm Still Nervous,' Says Soldier Who Shot Nicolae Ceausescu." *The Guardian*, December 7.

Guo, Xiaolin. 2001. "Land Expropriation and Rural Conflicts in China." *China Quarterly* 166: 422–439.

Hernández, Javier. 2018. "Young Activists Go Missing in China, Raising Fears of Crackdown." *New York Times*, November 11.

Hess, Steve. 2013. *Authoritarian Landscapes: Popular Mobilization and the Institutional Sources of Resilience in Nondemocracies*. Boston: Springer.

Heurlin, Christopher. 2017. *Responsive Authoritarianism: Land, Protests and Policymaking*. New York: Cambridge University Press.

Hollyer, James, Peter Rosendorff, and James Raymond Vreeland. 2015. "Transparency, Protest, and Autocratic Instability." *American Political Science Review* 109 (4): 764–784.

Hu, Jieren. 2011. "Grand Mediation in China: Mechanism and Application." *Asian Survey* 51 (6): 1063–1089.

Huang, Haifeng, Serra Baronbay, and Ling Huang. 2019. "Media, Protest Diffusion, and Authoritarian Resilience." *Political Science Research and Methods* 7 (1): 23–42.

Huang, Ronggui, and Ngai-ming Yip. 2012. "Internet and Activism in Urban China: A Case Study of Protests in Xiamen and Panyu." *Journal of Comparative Asian Development* 11 (2): 201–223.

Hurst, William. 2009. *The Chinese Worker after Socialism*. New York: Cambridge University Press.

Hurst, William, and Kevin O'Brien. 2002. "China's Contentious Pensioners." *China Quarterly* 170: 345–360.

Hyun, Ki Deuk, and Jinhee Kim. 2015. "The Role of New Media in Sustaining the Status Quo: Online Political Expression, Nationalism, and System Support in China." *Information, Communication & Society* 18 (7): 1–16.

Ieong, Meng U. 2016. "The Development of Grand Mediation and Its Implications for China's Regime Resilience: The Li Qin Mediation Office." *China Review* 16 (1): 95–119.

King, Gary, Jennifer Pan, and Margaret Roberts. 2013. "How Censorship in China Allows Government Criticism but Silences Collective Expression." *American Political Science Review* 107 (2): 1–18.

Kuang, Xianwen, and Christian Gobel. 2013. "Sustaining Collective Action in Urbanizing China." *China Quarterly* 216: 850–871

Kuo, Lily. 2018. "50 Student Activists Missing in China after Police Raid." *The Guardian*, August 24.

Kuran, Timur. 1991. "Now out of Never: The Element of Surprise in the East European Revolution of 1989." *World Politics* 44: 7–48.

Kurzman, Charles. 1996. "Structural Opportunity and Perceived Opportunity in Social-Movement Theory: The Iranian Revolution of 1979." *American Sociological Review* 61 (1): 153–170.

Lee, Ching Kwan. 2007. *Against the Law: Labor Protests in China's Rustbelt and Sunbelt*. Berkeley: University of California Press.

Lee, Ching Kwan, and Yonghong Zhang. 2013. "The Power of Instability: Unraveling the Microfoundations of Bargained Authoritarianism in China." *American Journal of Sociology* 118 (6): 1475–1508.

Lei, Ya-Wen. 2017. *The Contentious Public Sphere: Law, Media, and Authoritarian Rule in China*. Princeton, NJ: Princeton University Press.

Levitsky, Steven, and Lucan Way. 2010. *Competitive Authoritarianism: Hybrid Regimes after the Cold War*. New York: Cambridge University Press.

Li, Lianjiang, Mingxing Liu, and Kevin O'Brien. 2012. "Petitioning Beijing: The High Tide of 2003–2006." *China Quarterly* 210: 313–334.

Li, Lianjing and Kevin O'Brien. 2008. "Protest Leadership in Rural China." *China Quarterly* 193: 1–23.

Li, Yao. 2019. *Playing by the Informal Rules: Why the Chinese Regime Remains Stable Despite Rising Protests*. New York: Cambridge University Press.

Li, Yaoning. 2018. "Yi nüzi duoci feifa shangfang fan xunxin zishi zui zhong huoxing" (A woman was Convicted of Causing Disruption because of Illegal Petitions). http://sxxyzy.chinacourt.org/article/detail/2018/02/id/3207274.shtml.

Li Yukun. 2019. "Zhao Kezhi: fangfan diyu 'yanse geming'" (Preventing and Resisting "Color Revolution"). *Xin jingbao* (*New Beijing Post*), January 18.

Liang, Yucheng, and Zhang Haidong. 2016. "Report on the Investigation of the Middle-Level Stratum in Beijing, Shanghai, and Guangzhou." In Li Peilin, Chen Guangjin, and Zhang Yi (eds.), *Blue Book of Chinese Society 2016*. Beijing: Social Science Academic Press, pp. 189–218.

Lichbach, Mark. 1987. "The Puzzle of Aggregate Studies of Repression and Dissent." *The Journal of Conflict Resolution* 31 (2): 266–297.

Lieberthal, Kenneth, and Michel Oksenberg. 1988. *Policy Making in China: Leaders, Structures, and Processes*. Princeton, NJ: Princeton University Press.

Liu, Jun. 2013. "Mobile Communication, Popular Protests, and Citizenship in China." *Modern Asian Studies* 47 (3): 995–1018.

Liu, Sida, and Terence Halliday. 2016. *Criminal Defense in China: The Politics of Lawyers at Work*. New York: Cambridge University Press.

Liu, Yizhan. 2017. "Quanguo yi shixian shequ he jiedao renmin tiaojie weiyuanhui quan fugai" (The Mediation Committee Has Been Established across Residential Communities and Streets in the Country). *Sina*. http://news.sina.com.cn/sf/news/fzrd/2017-06-28/doc-ifyhmtcf3011530.shtml.

Lohmann, Susanne. 1994. "The Dynamics of Informational Cascades: The Monday Demonstrations in Leipzig, East Germany, 1989–91." *World Politics* 47 (1): 42–101.

Lorentzen, Peter. 2013. "Regularizing Rioting: Permitting Public Protest in an Authoritarian Regime." *Quarterly Journal of Political Science* 8 (2): 127–158.

Lu, Yao, and Ran Tao. 2017. "Organizational Structure and Collective Action: Lineage Networks, Semiautonomous Associations, and Collective Resistance in Rural China." *American Journal of Sociology* 122 (6): 1726–1774.

Lu, Zongshu and Qing Xuan. 2011. "Shangfangzhe tan yu zongli duihua xijie" (Petitioners Talked about the Details about Their Meeting with the Premier). *Southern Weekend*, January 28.

Luo, Qiangqiang, and Joel Andreas. 2016. "Using Religion to Resist Rural Dispossession: A Case Study of a Hui Muslim Community in Northwest China." *China Quarterly* 226: 477–498.

Luo, Ruiqing. 1994. *Lun renmin gong'an gongzuo* (On the People's Public Security). Beijing: The Masses Press.

Mai, Jun. 2019. "Chinese City Calls in Riot Police as Angry Investors Protest Outside P2P Lender's Headquarters." *South China Morning Post*, April 7.

McAdam, Doug. 1999. *Political Process and the Development of Black Insurgency 1930–1970*. Chicago: University of Chicago Press.

McAdam, Doug, and Richard Scott. 2005. "Organizations and Movements." In Gerald Davis, Doug McAdam, Richard Scott, and Mayer Zald (eds.), *Social Movements and Organization Theory*. New York: Cambridge University Press, pp. 4–40.

The Ministry of Education. 1989. *Jingxin dongpo de 56 Tian* (The Soul-Stirring 56 Days). Beijing: Land Press.

Myers, Steven Lee. 2020. "China Spins Tale That the U.S. Army Started the Coronavirus Epidemic." *New York Times*, March 17.

O'Brien, Kevin, and Neil Diamant. 2015. "Contentious Veterans: China's Retired Officers Speak Out." *Armed Forces & Society* 41 (3): 563–581.

O'Brien, Kevin, and Lianjiang Li. 2007. *Rightful Resistance in Rural China.* New York: Cambridge University Press.

Oberschall, Anthony. 1973. *Social Conflict and Social Movements.* Englewood Cliffs, NJ: Prentice-Hall.

Oi, Jean. 1989. *State and Peasant in Contemporary China: The Political Economy of Village Government.* Berkeley: University of California Press.

Ong, Lynette. 2018. "'Thugs-for-Hire': Subcontracting of State Coercion and State Capacity in China." *China Journal* 16 (3): 680–695.

Peng, Bing and Guan Shuang. 2011. "Jilin sheng 3 nian jiejue xinfang wenti 5 wan yu jian" (Jilin Province Solved 50,000 Cases within Three Years). *Workers Daily*, June 20.

Perry, Elizabeth. 1994. "Shanghai's Strike Wave of 1957." *China Quarterly* 137: 1–27.

2020. "Educated Acquiescence: How Academia Sustains Authoritarianism in China." *Theory and Society* 49: 1–22.

People's Daily. 2018. "Wangshang shouli xinfang zhidu shixing 5 nian lai wangshang xinfang liang zhan bi guoban" (Online Petitions Have Accounted for More Than Half of People's Petitions since the Online Petition System Was Established Five Years Ago). *People's Daily*, July 27. http://sc.people.com.cn/BIG5/n2/2018/0727/c345167-31865108.html.

People's Liberation Army Daily. 2016. "Tuijin jundui wangluo yulun gongzuo chuangxin fazhan" (Strengthening the Management of Online Public Opinion of the Military). *Jiefangjun bao* (*People's Liberation Army Daily*), June 26.

The Police Bureau of Shenzhen. 2006. "Xinshiqi yufang he chuzhi quntixing shijian de shijian yu sikao" (The Practice and Thoughts in Preventing and Managing the Mass Incidents in the New Era). *Gong'an Yanjiu* (*Policing Studies*) (10): 19–23.

Pun, Ngai. 2007. "Gendering the Dormitory Labor System: Production, Reproduction, and Migrant Labor in South China." *Feminist Economics* 13 (3–4): 239–258.

Read, Benjamin L. 2000. "Revitalizing the State's Urban 'Nerve Tips.'" *China Quarterly* 163: 806–820.

2012. *Roots of the State: Neighborhood Organization and Social Networks in Beijing and Taipei.* Stanford, CA: Stanford University Press.

Scott, James. 1976. *The Moral Economy of the Peasant: Rebellion and Subsistence in Southeast Asia*. New Haven, CT: Yale University Press.

1989. "Everyday Forms of Resistance." In Forrest Colburn (ed.), Everyday Forms of Peasant Resistance. Armonk, NY: M.E. Sharpe, pp. 3–33.

Sheng, Zhiming. 2019. *Cong xiaoqu dao shequ: Chengshi yezhu xingdong jiqi jieguo* (From Residential Community to Neighborhood Community: Homeowners' Action and Outcomes). Shanghai: Shanghai People's Press.

Shi, Fayong, and Yongshun Cai. 2006. "Disaggregating the State: Networks and Collective Action in Shanghai." *China Quarterly* 186: 314–332.

Shi, Jingtao. 2005. "Exodus Forced by Dam Under Way." *South China Morning Post*, December 13.

Shi, Tianjian. 1997. *Political Participation in Beijing*. Cambridge, MA: Harvard University Press.

Shirky, Clay. 2011. "The Political Power of Social Media: Technology, the Public Sphere, and Political Change." *Foreign Affairs* 90 (1): 28–41.

The Statistical Bureau. 2010. *China Compendium of Statistics 1949–2008*. Beijing: China Statistics Press.

Su, Yang, and Xin He. 2010. "Street as Courtroom: State Accommodation of Labor Protest in South China." *Law & Society Review* 44 (1): 157–184.

Svolik, Milan. 2012. *The Politics of Authoritarian Rule*. New York: Cambridge University Press.

Tang, Beibei. 2020. "Grid Governance in China's Urban Middle-Class Neighborhoods." *China Quarterly* 241: 43–61.

Tang, Wenfang. 2005. *Public Opinion and Political Trust in China*. Stanford, CA: Stanford University Press.

Tarrow, Sidney. 1998. *Power in Movement*. New York: Cambridge University Press.

Teiwes, Frederick. 1987. "Establishment and Consolidation of the New Regime." In Denis Twitchett and John Fairbank (eds.), *The Cambridge History of China, vol. 14*. Cambridge: Cambridge University Press, pp. 51–121.

Teiwes, Frederick, and Warren Sun. 2004. "The First Tiananmen Incident Revisited: Elite Politics and Crisis Management at the End of the Maoist Era." *Pacific Affairs* 77 (2): 211–235.

Tilly, Charles. 1978. *From Mobilization to Revolution*. Reading, MA: Addison-Wesley.

Tomba, Luigi. 2015. *The Government Next Door: Neighborhood Politics in Urban China*. Ithaca, NY: Cornell University Press.

Tong, James. 2009. *Revenge of the Forbidden City: The Suppression of the Falungong in China, 1999–2008*. New York: Oxford University Press.

References

Tu, Chonghang, and Xu, Oulu. 2013. "Wangluo yuqing fenxishi cheng guanfang renke zhiye, congye zhe da 200 wan" (Analysts of Online Public Opinion Are Accepted by the Government, and the Number Reaches Two Million). *Xin jingbao* (*New Beijing Post*), October 13.

Walder, Andrew. 1986. *Communist Neo-Traditionalism: Work and Authority in Chinese Industry*. Berkeley: University of California Press.

2009. "Unruly Stability: Why China's Regime Has Staying Power." *Current History* 108: 257–263.

Wang, Juan. 2012. "Shifting Boundaries between the State and Society: Village Cadres as New Activists in Collective Petitioning." *China Quarterly* 211: 697–717.

2015. "Managing Social Stability: The Perspective of a Local Government in China." *Journal of East Asian Studies* 15 (1): 1–25.

Wang, Shaoguang. 1995. *Failure of Charisma: The Cultural Revolution in Wuhan*. Hong Kong: Oxford University Press.

Wang, Yuhua, and Carl Minzner. 2015. "The Rise of the Chinese Security State." *China Quarterly* 222: 339–359.

Washington Post Editorial Board. 2018. "A Professor Dared Tell the Truth in China – And Was Fired." *Washington Post*, August 23.

Weaver, Kent. 1986. "The Politics of Blame Avoidance." *Journal of Public Policies* 6 (4): 371–398.

Whiting, Susan. 2004. "The Cadre Evaluation System at the Grass Roots: The Paradox of Party Rule." In Barry Naughton and Dali Yang (ed.), *Holding China Together: Diversity and National Integration in the Post-Deng Era*. New York: Cambridge University Press, pp. 101–119.

Whyte, Martin. 2010. *Myth of the Social Volcano: Perceptions of Inequality and Distributive Injustice in Contemporary China*. Stanford, CA: Stanford University Press.

Wintrobe, Ronald. 1998. *The Political Economy of Dictatorship*. New York: Cambridge University Press.

Wong, Linda, and Bernard Poon. 2005. "From Serving Neighbors to Recontrolling Urban Society: The Transformation of China's Community Policy." *China Information* 19 (3): 413–442.

Wright, Teresa. 2010. *Accepting Authoritarianism: State-society Relations in China's Reform Era*. Stanford, CA: Stanford University Press.

Xia, Ying. 2019. "The Dual Logic of the Petition System and the 'Non-Administrative Petitions': The Case of Repeated Collective Petitions in City A." *Zhengzhi Xue Yanjiu* (*Political Research*) 4: 102–128.

Xie, Lei, and Hein-Anton van der Heijden. 2010. "Environmental Movements and Political Opportunities: The Case of China." *Social Movement Studies* 9 (1): 51–68.

Yan, Alice. 2018. "Violent Veterans Rally in China Leads to 10 Arrests." *South China Morning Post*, December 10.

Yan, Fameng. 2018. "Zuigao fayuan: zai fei xinfang changsuo tichu xinfang shixiang, bushuyu yifa weiquan" (The Supreme Court: Petitioning in Wrong Places Is Not Lawful), www.sohu.com/a/253470854_260282.

Yan, Xiaojun. 2016. "Patrolling Harmony: Pre-Emptive Authoritarianism and the Preservation of Stability in W County." *Journal of Contemporary China* 25 (99): 406–421.

Yang, Zheyu. 2012. "Xi Jinping liangxiang: Zeren, tiaozhan, yu jingxing" (Xi Jinping's Debut: Responsibility, Challenges, and Vigilance," https://opinion .caixin.com/2012-11-15/100461134.html.

Ying, Shusheng. 2011. "Dayuejin' qianhou de shehui kongzhi" (Social Control before and after the Great Leap Forward). *Yanhuang chunqiu* (*China through the Ages*) 4: 8–12.

Zhang, Han. 2015. "Party Building in Urban Business Districts: Organizational Adaptation of the Chinese Communist Party." *Journal of Contemporary China* 24 (94): 644–664.

Zhang, Han, and Jennifer Pan. 2019. "CASM: A Deep-Learning Approach for Identifying Collective Action Events with Text and Image Data from Social Media." *Sociological Methodology* 49 (1): 1–57.

Zhang, Liang, and Perry Link (eds.). 2001. *The Tiananmen Papers*. New York: Public Affairs.

Zhang, Phoebe. 2019. "Chinese Parents Clash with Police as They Demand Answers over Children's Vaccine Scandal." *South China Morning Post*, January 11.

Zhang, Wu. 2015. "Leadership, Organization and Moral Authority: Explaining Peasant Militancy in Contemporary China." *China Journal* 73: 59–83.

Zhou, Xueguang, and Yun Ai. 2016 "Bases of Governance and Forms of Resistance: The Case of Rural China." In David Courpasson and Steven Vallas (eds.), *The SAGE Handbook of Resistance*. Thousand Oaks, CA: Sage Publications, p, pp. 443–460.

Zweig, David. 2000. "The 'Externalities of Development': Can New Political Institutions Manage Rural Conflict?" In Elizabeth Perry and Mark Selden (eds.), *Chinese Society: Change, Conflict and Resistance*. London: Routledge, pp. 120–142.

Cambridge Elements ≡

Politics and Society in East Asia

Erin Aeran Chung
Johns Hopkins University

Erin Aeran Chung is the Charles D. Miller Associate Professor of East Asian Politics in the Department of Political Science at the Johns Hopkins University. She specializes in East Asian political economy, international migration, and comparative racial politics. She is the author of *Immigration and Citizenship in Japan* (Cambridge, 2010, 2014; Japanese translation, Akashi Shoten, 2012) and *Immigrant Incorporation in East Asian Democracies* (Cambridge, 2020). Her research has been supported by grants from the Academy of Korean Studies, the Japan Foundation, the Japan Foundation Center for Global Partnership, the Social Science Research Council, and the American Council of Learned Societies.

Mary Alice Haddad
Wesleyan University

Mary Alice Haddad is the John E. Andrus Professor of Government, East Asian Studies, and Environmental Studies at Wesleyan University. Her research focuses on democracy, civil society, and environmental politics in East Asia as well as city diplomacy around the globe. A Fulbright and Harvard Academy scholar, Haddad is author of *Effective Advocacy: Lessons from East Asia's Environmentalists* (MIT, 2021), *Building Democracy in Japan* (Cambridge, 2012), and *Politics and Volunteering in Japan* (Cambridge, 2007), and co-editor of *Greening East Asia* (University of Washington, 2021), and *NIMBY is Beautiful* (Berghahn Books, 2015). She has published in journals such as Comparative Political Studies, Democratization, Journal of Asian Studies, and Nonprofit and Voluntary Sector Quarterly, with writing for the public appearing in the Asahi Shimbun, the Hartford Courant, and the South China Morning Post.

Benjamin L. Read
University of California, Santa Cruz

Benjamin L. Read is a professor of Politics at the University of California, Santa Cruz. His research has focused on local politics in China and Taiwan, and he also writes about issues and techniques in field research. He is author of *Roots of the State: Neighborhood Organization and Social Networks in Beijing and Taipei* (Stanford, 2012), coauthor of *Field Research in Political Science: Practices and Principles* (Cambridge, 2015), and co-editor of *Local Organizations and Urban Governance in East and Southeast Asia: Straddling State and Society* (Routledge, 2009). His work has appeared in journals such as Comparative Political Studies, Comparative Politics, the Journal of Conflict Resolution, the China Journal, the China Quarterly, and the Washington Quarterly, as well as several edited books.

About the Series

The Cambridge Elements series on Politics and Society in East Asia offers original, multidisciplinary contributions on enduring and emerging issues in the dynamic region of East Asia by leading scholars in the field. Suitable for general readers and specialists alike, these short, peer-reviewed volumes examine common challenges and patterns within the region while identifying key differences between countries. The series consists of two types of contributions: 1) authoritative field surveys of established concepts and themes that offer roadmaps for further research; and 2) new research on emerging issues that challenge conventional understandings of East Asian politics and society. Whether focusing on an individual country or spanning the region, the contributions in this series connect regional trends with points of theoretical debate in the social sciences and will stimulate productive interchanges among students, researchers, and practitioners alike.

Cambridge Elements $^{\equiv}$

Politics and Society in East Asia

Elements in the series

The East Asian Covid-19 Paradox
Yves Tiberghien

State, Society and Markets in North Korea
Andrew Yeo

The Digital Transformation and Japan's Political Economy
Ulrike Schaede and Kay Shimizu

Japan as a Global Military Power: New Capabilities, Alliance Integration, Bilateralism-Plus
Christopher W. Hughes

State and Social Protests in China
Yongshun Cai and Chih-Jou Jay Chen

A full series listing is available at: www.cambridge.org/EPEA

www.ingramcontent.com/pod-product-compliance
Ingram Content Group UK Ltd.
Pitfield, Milton Keynes, MK11 3LW, UK
UKHW020455010325
455719UK00016B/591